OUR HOUSE

Los Angeles Daily News

THE LOS ANGELES RAMS' AMAZING 2021 CHAMPIONSHIP SEASON

This book is available in quantity at special discounts for your group or organization. For further information, contact:

Triumph Books LLC
814 North Franklin Street
Chicago, Illinois 60610
Phone: (312) 337-0747
www.triumphbooks.com

Printed in U.S.A.
ISBN: 978-1- 63727-125-4

Southern California News Group
Ron Hasse, President & Publisher
Bill Van Laningham, Vice President, Marketing
Frank Pine, Executive Editor
Tom Moore, Executive Sports Editor
Michele Cardon and Dean Musgrove, Photo Editors

Content packaged by Mojo Media, Inc.
Joe Funk: Editor
Jason Hinman: Creative Director

Production Manager: Kris Anstrats
Triumph Books Thanks You for 20+ Years of Service!

Los Angeles Daily News: David Crane

CONTENTS

INTRO

The Rams Finish Off Their Comeback to L.A.

By Todd Harmonson

Excess was the order of the day.

From the outrageous prices simply to park, let alone to get in SoFi Stadium, to the non-stop stream of celebrities who suddenly were diehard fans and the dream Los Angeles halftime show, there was little that was subtle about Super Bowl LVI.

Then Rams owner Stan Kroenke accepted the Vince Lombardi Trophy, the second in the franchise's history but the first representing Los Angeles, and delivered perhaps the ultimate in understatement.

"As far as building this stadium, I think it turned out all right," Kroenke said.

Kroenke's move to bring the Rams back to Los Angeles in 2016 after more than two decades in St. Louis capped its comeback with a 23-20 Rams triumph over the Cincinnati Bengals in Super Bowl LVI.

His $5.5 billion palace – next to where the Lakers once collected championships at the Forum – was packed with 70,048 who witnessed the Rams become only the second NFL team to win a Super Bowl at home.

Nothing like this seemed possible when then-Rams owner Georgia Frontiere took the team from Anaheim following the 1994 season or even when they returned and sputtered to a 4-12 record in a forgettable 2016 season at the Coliseum.

In between, there were years of disappointment for local fans who simply wanted their team, and some couldn't even bring themselves to celebrate the franchise's first championship in Super Bowl XXXIV because it was for St. Louis. After that one, Frontiere was anything but subtle when she said the victory

proved the Rams did the right thing by moving.

This one, however, was all about the Los Angeles area.

The Rams gave the region another major championship following the Dodgers' and Lakers' triumphs in 2020, but this one L.A. fans expect to be able to celebrate in grand style.

"There's something really powerful about being a part of something bigger than yourself," said Rams coach Sean McVay, who reached his second Super Bowl in five seasons and won his first at only 36 years old.

Rams superstar defensive lineman Aaron Donald started with the team in St. Louis and, appropriately, finished off Sunday's victory when he pressured Bengals quarterback Joe Burrow into an incomplete pass on Cincinnati's final play.

"I've been here eight years," Donald said. "A lot of ups and downs."

The Rams experienced one of those downs in Super Bowl LIII, when they came up short against the New England Patriots and lost, 13-3. They missed the playoffs the following season and were eliminated in the second round of the postseason last year.

As much as they went all-in to win this season by loading up with veteran talent, it was anything but a given that they would win the championship.

"We fought through adversity when I first got here," said Rams linebacker Von Miller, who came to the Rams on Nov. 1 in a trade from the Denver Broncos. "We lost three in a row.

"We've got a team full of fighters."

Another newcomer this season was quarterback

Mary J. Blige was part of an unforgettable halftime show and an apt one for a Super Bowl in Los Angeles, also headlined by Dr. Dre, Snoop Dogg, Kendrick Lamar, and Eminem. (Los Angeles Daily News: David Crane)

Matthew Stafford, who was acquired in a blockbuster trade in the offseason with the Detroit Lions for former Rams No. 1 pick Jared Goff – the player who was supposed to be their future when they returned to L.A. – and draft picks.

Stafford battled through Sunday's game and led the Rams' comeback in the final minutes, capped by a 1-yard touchdown pass to Super Bowl MVP Cooper Kupp with 1:25 to play.

"This is a long time coming for a lot of guys," said Stafford, who never won a playoff game with the Lions but led the Rams to four postseason victories in five weeks.

Things definitely improved for Stafford with his move to Los Angeles, which embraced its moment against the Bengals in every way possible.

The unseasonably hot February Sunday settled to a nice 82 degrees at kickoff.

Dr. Dre gathered some of his closest friends, including Long Beach native Snoop Dogg, for a halftime show that immediately moved into the discussion – after Prince's in 2007, of course – of the all-time best.

Celebrities were spotted all over SoFi Stadium, as expected, but few from movies or music garnered the applause saved for some of Los Angeles' greatest athletes. Jennifer Lopez was greeted warmly, for instance. But it was nothing compared to what Dodgers pitcher Clayton

Kershaw and Lakers legends Kareem Abdul-Jabbar, Magic Johnson and Shaquille O'Neal heard.

Scalpers didn't bother trying to sell tickets outside SoFi Stadium; those were going for thousands of dollars on the secondary market. They were busy hawking coveted parking spots for hundreds of dollars, some at local businesses and others on neighborhood lawns.

There were opportunists pushing liquid refreshments at high prices for the crowds that made their way in the heat toward SoFi's entrances, and they were matched in their numbers by those offering street-corner salvation.

Inside the stadium, the crowd was pretty evenly split between Rams fans who had endured their years of pain and Bengals fans who had experienced worse in support of a franchise that was the laughingstock of the NFL for a long time.

They all witnessed a stellar game that could've gone either way. The Rams and Bengals were evenly matched and delivered at a high level.

The Rams, however, simply had enough to pull out the most important victory in the L.A. version of the franchise's history and complete a comeback from much more than a fourth-quarter deficit.

"To be able to do it in the house that Mr. Kroenke built was really special," McVay said. ∎

Rams 23, Bengals 20
February 13, 2022 • Inglewood, California

'THAT'S WHY THEY'RE WORLD CHAMPIONS'

Rams Beat Bengals, Win Super Bowl on Late Touchdown

By Kevin Modesti

For generations of Los Angeles Rams fans, it was a dream. For owner Stan Kroenke, it was a blueprint. For general manager Les Snead, it was a gamble. For coach Sean McVay, it was a game plan. For players like Aaron Donald, it was a bucket-list goal.

At precisely 7 p.m. in Inglewood, it became a fact.

The L.A. Rams are Super Bowl champions.

It came true in a dramatic and fitting way, with quarterback Matthew Stafford throwing a 1-yard touchdown pass to wide receiver Cooper Kupp to give the Rams the lead over the Cincinnati Bengals with 1:25 to play.

The defense finished the job in equally trademark fashion, with Donald pressuring Bengals quarterback Joe Burrow into an incomplete pass on fourth-and-1 near midfield to clinch the 23-20 victory in front of 70,048 fans.

After Stafford took one snap and knelt to run out the last 39 seconds of the 35th fourth-quarter comeback of his career, Rams players and coaches surged off the sideline to celebrate in a cloud of confetti.

"For the offense to be able to find a way, and then Aaron to be able to finish it off," Rams coach Sean McVay said, "it's poetic."

Kupp was named Most Valuable Player of the game, capping a season in which he led NFL receivers in catches, yards and touchdowns and was named the league's Offensive Player of the Year.

But much of the joy was for older players winning their first championships as a team called the L.A. Rams won the Super Bowl for the first time: Donald, the great defensive tackle whose Hall of Fame resume lacked only a championship. Left tackle Andrew Whitworth, perhaps playing his final game at age 40. Safety Eric Weddle, who ended a two-year retirement to help the Rams in the playoffs.

"Mission completed," said Donald, who had two of the Rams' seven sacks.

None of them would have reached the pinnacle without Stafford.

The 34-year-old quarterback brought over from the Lions in a trade 11 months prior went from never having won a playoff game to winning it all, and completing it in the most challenging way possible.

"The last drive was a great drive, one I'll never forget," said Stafford, who praised McVay for aggressive play-calling.

Nobody in the mixed crowd of Rams blue and Bengals orange will either.

Cooper Kupp hauls in the go-ahead touchdown late in the fourth quarter of Super Bowl LVI. Kupp had eight catches for 92 yards and two touchdowns on his way to winning Super Bowl MVP. (Los Angeles Daily News: Keith Birmingham)

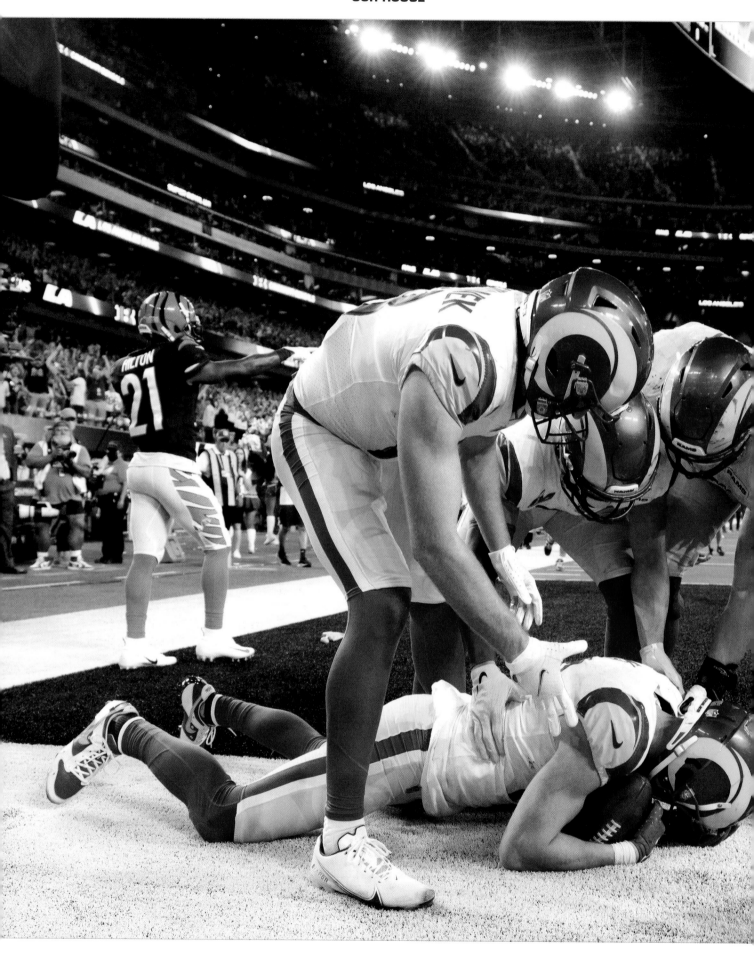

The Rams got the ball on a punt with 6:13 to play, trailing by four points and perhaps thinking of a blown extra point in the first half.

They started with a 9-yard pass to little-used tight end Brycen Hopkins, helping replace injured Tyler Higbee. A 7-yard run by Kupp converted a fourth-and-1. Stafford went back to Hopkins for 6 to go across the 50. Strikes to Kupp for 22 and 8 yards got the Rams to the 16, and a run by Cam Akers put them at the 8 at the two-minute warning.

The Bengals made mistakes as they played in their first Super Bowl in a generation. Defensive holding turned a third-down incompletion into first down at the 4. After offsetting penalties canceled a Kupp catch in the end zone, pass interference on another missed pass to Kupp put the ball at the 1. Stafford came up short on a first-down sneak, and then went to Kupp once again.

It was a 15-play, 79-yard drive taking nearly five minutes.

The game wasn't over. Burrow and Ja'Marr Chase got the ball across the 50. But on fourth and 1 with :43 on the giant SoFi Stadium video screen, Donald wrapped up the young quarterback and forced a wild pass.

Now it was over.

The game had been like the Rams' season, brilliant to begin with, worrisome in the middle, as good as it could be at the end.

The underdog Bengals looked set to take charge on the first two plays of the second half.

The Bengals took the lead for the first time at 17-13 on a first-down pass play from Burrow to Tee Higgins covering 75 yards.

TV replays showed Higgins grabbing Jalen Ramsey by the face mask, pulling down the All-Pro cornerback as they fought for the ball. Higgins caught it at about the Rams' 35 and was untouched to the end zone.

The no-call of a face-mask penalty couldn't be reviewed under NFL rules.

On the next snap, Stafford threw to Ben Skowronek, who was replacing injured Odell Beckham Jr. The ball glanced

It was appropriate that Cooper Kupp caught what turned out to be the game-winning touchdown, as he was dominant all season, including winning the NFL's Offensive Player of the Year award. (Los Angeles Daily News: Keith Birmingham)

Linebacker Ernest Jones (50) celebrates after sacking Cincinnati's Joe Burrow, one of seven sacks for the Los Angeles defense in the game. (Los Angeles Daily News: Keith Birmingham)

off the rookie's hands and straight to safety Jessie Bates. The Bengals had the ball at the Rams' 31.

"A lot of teams would have folded," McVay said.

The damage from Stafford's second interception of the day was limited by two sacks by Donald, among the Rams' seven sacks of Burrow, forcing a field goal that put the Bengals up 20-13.

It turned into an exchange of field goals when a third-down trick play resulted in an overthrown pass from Kupp to Stafford, and it was Bengals 20, Rams 16.

The game kicked off on an 82-degree afternoon, the Bengals seeking their first Super Bowl victory on their third try, the Rams seeking their first Super Bowl trophy as an L.A. team after winning one in their St. Louis years and two mid-century NFL championships.

The Rams had extra incentive to win at their home stadium, built at a cost of $5 billion by Kroenke, and to do it in the season Snead went "all in" by acquiring Stafford and adding Beckham and linebacker Von Miller in a show of urgency.

"I think building this stadium turned out all right," Kroenke said as he accepted the Lombardi Trophy.

The game went the Rams' way early.

The defense held the Bengals without a first down on their first two series, rookie linebacker Ernest Jones deflecting Joe Burrow's pass on fourth and 1 at the Rams' 49.

Stafford took advantage of the field position, hitting Kupp for a 20-yard catch and run into the red zone, and then throwing a perfect pass to Beckham behind a Cincinnati cornerback in the right corner of the end zone for a 17-yard touchdown.

The defense gave up a 46-yard pass from Burrow to Chase, who got behind Ramsey and took the Bengals to the Rams' 11. But then it tightened, with Von Miller deflecting a pass and Ramsey breaking up a third-down pass at the goal line. Evan McPherson's 29-yard field goal cut the lead to 7-3.

The Rams quickly went 75 yards. Beckham took a pass 35 yards into Bengals territory, and Darrell Henderson came out of the backfield to catch a 25-yarder up the left sideline.

Franchise legend Aaron Donald celebrates after the Rams clinched Super Bowl LVI on their home turf. (Los Angeles Daily News: Keith Birmingham)

On second down from the 11, Stafford and Kupp made it look easy, play-action helping the NFL's leading receiver get open crossing left to right in the end zone.

It was 13-3 after a messed-up exchange from long snapper Matt Orzech to holder Johnny Hekker kept Matt Gay from trying the extra point.

Hoping to slow down Bengals running back Joe Mixon and mount a rush on the often-sacked Burrow, the Rams' defense did neither often in the first half.

After the Kupp touchdown, the Bengals marched 75 yards in 12 plays, most of them involving Mixon. He carried and caught passes to help Cincinnati get inside the Rams' 10. Then he took a pitch from Burrow and threw a pass to Higgins, who got away from Nick Scott in the right corner of the end zone to cut the Rams' lead to 13-10.

Ahead on the scoreboard, the Rams were down in the injury tent, Beckham having been helped off the field after quickly grabbing his left knee as he dropped a pass over the middle without being hit.

The loss of Beckham made it easier for the Bengals' defense to focus on Kupp, but he was able to catch eight of the 10 passes Stafford threw him for 92 yards and the two touchdowns.

As had happened in the Rams' last-minute drive to win the second-round playoff game against the Buccaneers, and their late drive to the winning field goal in the NFC championship game against the 49ers, they counted on Stafford and Kupp when it mattered most.

"You talk about guys being at their best when their best is required," McVay said. "That's why they're world champions." ■

The midseason acquisition of Von Miller paid off in a big way in Super Bowl LVI, as Miller pressured Joe Burrow all game and finished with two sacks. [AP Images]

General manager Les Snead (left), Matthew Stafford (center) and Cooper Kupp (right) celebrate the first Super Bowl title in franchise history while based in L.A. (Los Angeles Daily News: Keith Birmingham)

TALKING THE TALK

Aaron Donald Revels in First Super Bowl Victory

By Kyle Goon | February 13, 2022

Quiet leadership has its time and place. Aaron Donald has done things that way for years, arriving to practice early and leaving late, in his own words "working my ass off" and silently influencing teammates to do the same.

There is a time to hold words in, to let the work speak for you. But at the close of Super Bowl LVI, it was time for the world to hear Aaron Donald finally talk his talk.

Moments after ripping Cincinnati Bengals quarterback Joe Burrow to the turf on fourth down, sending the ball tumbling out of his hands like a discarded toy, Donald popped off his helmet, raised his arms and shouted at the top of his lungs: "Ring me!"

The 30-year-old Rams defensive lineman has done everything the right way with a soft-spoken, diligent approach. Now after eight seasons, Donald can say anything he wants.

He's a Super Bowl champion after a road that far surpassed even his own dreams.

"I would have never thought in a million years I'd be sitting here right now, with the success I've had in a short amount of time in this league," he said. "You put the body of work in, a lot of good things can happen out of that."

It certainly didn't feel like a short wait.

Rams safety Eric Weddle, who knows what it is to hold out hope for years, was among the first to grab the helmet-less Donald in a joyful embrace as the Rams got the ball back with 39 seconds left, knowing that the elusive L.A. championship was now firmly in their grasp.

But throughout this season, the entire Rams team has spouted how, as much as any player on the roster, Donald gave them the motivation to win it all. Von Miller, who was the MVP of Super Bowl 50 with the Denver Broncos, said he wanted to see Donald have his championship moment.

The 13th overall pick in 2014 out of Pittsburgh, Donald is one of the few holdovers from the St. Louis era of the Rams. Before the team returned to Los Angeles in 2016, before Coach Sean McVay was hired, before the Rams went to the Super Bowl in 2019, Donald was grinding, establishing himself as not just a franchise star, but a fixture, steady and reliable. His 98 sacks and 23 forced fumbles are a tribute to his impact, yet don't really say enough about the future Hall of Famer.

"Guys like him are why you coach: He's elevated everybody," McVay said. "The epitome of greatness is making everybody you're around and every situation better. That's exactly what Aaron does."

There was something painfully unforgettable about how the Rams' last postseason ended: Donald wiping tear-filled eyes in the frigid Green Bay winter, unable to stop his team from getting run over by the Packers

Cornerback Jalen Ramsey lifts Aaron Donald in celebration as the Rams clinched a thrilling Super Bowl LVI win.
(Los Angeles Daily News: Keith Birmingham)

in the divisional round. His ribs were aching, keeping him from making a difference, but what was even more obvious was that his heart was broken by yet another playoff run cut short.

The same was true in the Super Bowl as was true that day: If the Rams were to win the game, Donald would have to be a starring player.

For a half, he was confined to the wings of the stage. When the Bengals finally got themselves into the end zone in the second quarter, Donald was a spectator, well-blocked out of the play and biting on the trick play to Joe Mixon like everyone else in the stadium. He could only watch when receiver Tee Higgins shook Jalen Ramsey (with a little help from a facemask) and dashed for a 75-yard touchdown to give the Bengals the lead to start the third quarter.

Moments later, a Stafford pass bounced off of Ben Skowronek and into the hands of Chidobe Awuzie. After leading most of the first half, the Rams suddenly needed some kind of spark, with the Bengals taking over at their 31-yard line, to keep from sliding into the abyss.

That was when Donald truly emerged, sacking Burrow twice on the drive and limiting Cincinnati to just a field goal despite its advantageous position. On the second of these sacks, Donald plowed straight through guard Hakeem Adeniji to wrap his thick arms around Burrow, then flexed his arms, like a grizzly bear hunkered over his latest meal.

It was the start of a second-half deluge of pressure on Burrow, who from then on saw Rams pass rushers wedging through every crease. Six of L.A.'s Super Bowl record-tying seven sacks came during the second half. Without many of their offensive playmakers, including receiver Odell Beckham Jr. getting injured midway through the game, the Rams' offense needed all the support it could get from that side of the ball.

On the final play when the Bengals were looking to throw, McVay beckoned reporters to go back and listen to him mic'd up: "I said, 'Aaron is going to close the game out right here. He is the effing man.'"

Even before playing a snap, NFL observers were buzzing about Donald after NBC commentator Rodney Harrison sent a rumor flying on the broadcast: "He also told me this: If he wins a Super Bowl, there's a strong possibility that he could walk away from the game and retire."

Donald's legacy is set: He's an eight-time Pro Bowler and a three-time NFL Defensive Player of the Year. His gold jacket is already waiting in Canton. Whenever the Rams get around to erecting statues outside of SoFi Stadium, he'll be the first man cast in bronze.

But whatever he decides to do, Donald has no more what-ifs, could-have-beens, if-onlys. He won't be one of the greatest to never win a Super Bowl; he'll simply be one of the greatest ever. As he ran off the field, Donald showed the world his ring finger, pointing to where the last piece he had been chasing finally would slide into place.

Donald declined to comment on Harrison's report, saying he was enjoying the moment that he got to share with his wife and three children, who spent a good chunk of the postgame celebration making snow angels in the blizzard of blue-and-gold confetti mounting on the turf.

Eight-year-old Jaeda Donald clutched a palmful of that confetti as she stood aside him on the postgame dais. Her father explained that three years ago in Super Bowl LIII, he failed to deliver a promise that they would get to bask in it.

"Wasn't that fun?" Aaron asked. Jaeda enthusiastically agreed.

If that was the final mission for Donald and the Rams, he's delivered on every promise he could reasonably be expected to keep. ∎

Super Bowl LVI was the culmination of what is sure to be a Hall of Fame career for Aaron Donald. Appropriately, he had two huge sacks in the second half and helped force an incompletion on fourth down on the final drive for the Bengals, clinching that elusive Super Bowl ring. (Los Angeles Daily News: David Crane)

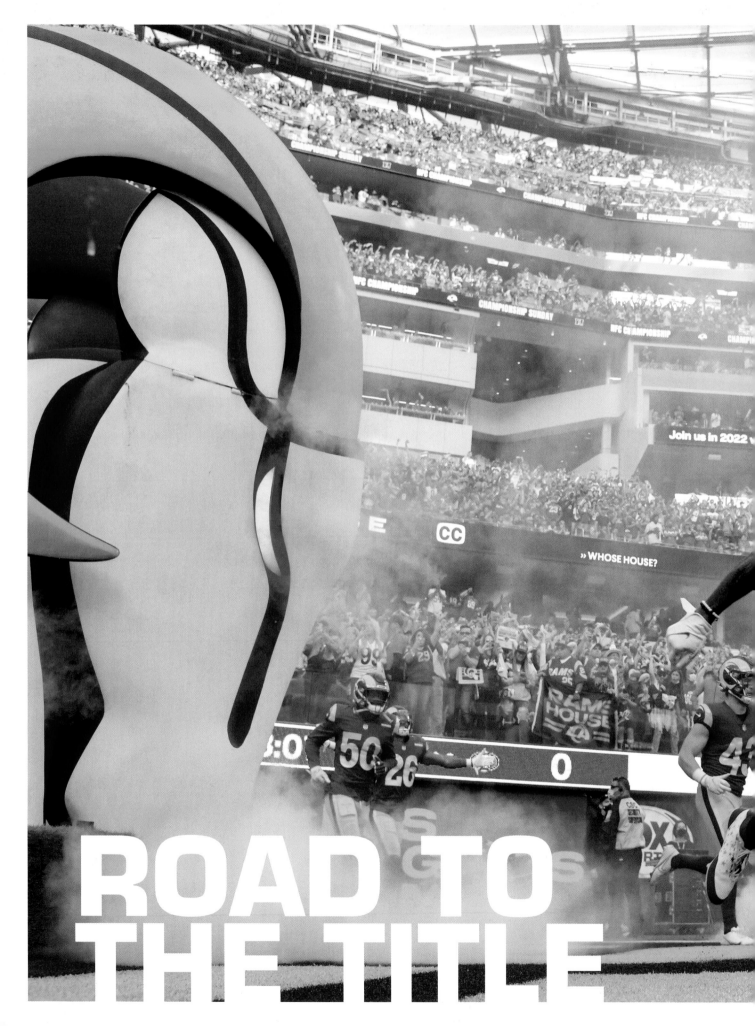

ROAD TO THE TITLE

9

QUARTERBACK

MATTHEW STAFFORD

Rams See New QB as a High-Mileage Survivor

March 19, 2021 | By Mark Whicker

Among the great euphemisms of our time is "pre-owned." Nobody wants to admit buying a used car. Much better to go pre-owned. Better yet, "experienced."

The Rams are getting Matthew Stafford, 33, at the 100,000-mile mark. Few quarterbacks make it there.

They had a first-overall choice in Jared Goff. He took them, or maybe they took him, to a Super Bowl. Goff never was as bad as his critics claim, but suddenly in 2020 one of his critics became Sean McVay, which is slightly worse than getting a thumbs-down from Roger Ebert.

The Rams did not know Goff, 26, would develop an aversion to pressure or a habit of throwing the ball to the wrong jersey near the end zone. That was not in the owner's manual.

But look around. Carson Wentz was the second player picked in that 2016 draft and for a while he was Rocky. Then, after injuries and ineffectiveness and a poorly disguised dispute with the bosses, he was W.C. Fields. When Wentz signed with Indianapolis and had his media conference call, he stipulated that he wouldn't answer questions from Philly.

Mitchell Trubisky was the second pick in 2017. He became a starter in Chicago and is now a backup in Buffalo.

Sam Darnold was the third pick in 2018. The Jets think they might box him up and ship him somewhere.

Jameis Winston and Marcus Mariota were the 1-2 picks in 2015. Jackson started in Tampa Bay and was the backup in New Orleans last year. Mariota started in Tennessee and is now with the Raiders (though he could be traded or released soon).

Quarterback Drama rages like never before. Seattle and Russell Wilson are no longer adjoined. The 49ers don't know what to do with Jimmy Garoppolo. Deshaun Watson has foresworn Houston, although it's a little more complicated than that. Drew Lock is no lock to be Denver's guy.

Of the first-overall picks at quarterback, Baker Mayfield, Kyler Murray and Stafford have been the only

Of the many reasons the Rams wanted Matthew Stafford to replace Jared Goff, his ability to connect on the deep throw was chief among them. (Los Angeles Daily News: Keith Birmingham)

real survivors over the past 11 years. The Rams have noticed that. The fact that Stafford was a 2009 model was a selling point.

"Repetition is the mother of learning the right way," McVay said. "The game makes sense to him. Like Pat Mahomes and Aaron Rodgers, he can manipulate the coverage with his eyes and then deliver from different arm slots. I respect the lens that he sees the game through.

"Plus, he has a humility that's refreshing."

Stafford earned that honestly, on bruising afternoons in Detroit's Ford Field. Year after year after quarterback coach after head coach after offensive coordinator, he fought the good fight in the roughhouse NFC North, almost always without reward. The Lions had eight losing seasons in Stafford's dozen years of dirt roads.

Yet Stafford avoided the incessant finger-pointing that besets most quarterbacks. Detroit is demanding. You could attend an NBA Finals game in 2005 and see a "Fire Joey" banner, referring to quarterback Harrington. Maybe Lions fans had seen so many woeful quarterbacks that they didn't want to run off a good one. There was respect, and maybe relief, when he finally said he'd had enough.

Meanwhile, the Rams have shed significant players to get salary cap-compliant. Half of a brilliant secondary is gone, and so are defensive tackle Michael Brockers and backup running back Malcolm Brown and linebacker Samson Ebukam. That's part of business. Stafford's ability to take his position from "good to great," as General Manager Les Snead said, is enhanced by the retention of most of the rest of the offense. Did the Rams have trouble getting deep? Yes, but maybe Stafford's deep-space arm will solve that, not a sprinting receiver.

Snead was with Atlanta in 2009 and he knew the Falcons weren't in position to get Stafford. He drove to Stafford's Pro Day at Georgia anyway.

The Rams had a hunch that Matthew Stafford would excel with a fresh start in L.A. and he paid it off with championship results. (Los Angeles Daily News: David Crane)

"It was 50 miles from our office in Flowery Branch to Athens," Snead said, "and you could probably count on getting pulled over, on that road. But I still remember what he did. It's the best one I've seen from a quarterback standpoint. It's stamped in my mind to this day. When his wrist came around and the ball came out, you could feel it."

Nick Jones is an assistant offensive line coach with the Rams. He was the center at Georgia when Stafford appeared.

"All we heard about was this kid from Texas," Jones said. "I didn't understand the magnitude of signing him. But then I saw him throw it for the first time. I said, 'Whoa. Damn. This kid's pretty good.'"

Now Matthew Stafford is no longer a kid. That, it turns out, is probably why he's here. ■

Opposite: Matthew Stafford embraced the winning culture established by the Rams, a sharp contrast to eight losing seasons in his time with the Lions. (Los Angeles Daily News: Keith Birmingham) Above: Stafford's versatility as a passer compares to some of the best quarterbacks in the game, including Patrick Mahomes and Aaron Rodgers. (Los Angeles Daily News: Keith Birmingham)

Rams 34, Bears 14
September 12, 2021 • Inglewood, California

OFF AND GUNNING

Rams QB Matthew Stafford's Long Strikes Beat Bears

By Kevin Modesti

The Rams' toughest opponent Sunday night might not have been the Chicago Bears but the high expectations of SoFi Stadium's first regular-season crowd.

Matthew Stafford's arrival in a trade last winter had fans picturing the Rams riding an explosive passing game to a home-field Super Bowl next February.

Could they encourage such dreams?

Indeed they could, and without delay. Stafford connected with Van Jefferson for a 67-yard touchdown pass before much of the crowd of 70,445 was seated. Then he hit Cooper Kupp for a 56-yard touchdown before everybody was back from halftime.

The Rams handled expectations and the Bears in a 34-14 victory that was their fifth opening-game win in Sean McVay's five years as coach.

"It was exactly what we wanted," McVay said.

Stafford finished 20 for 26 for 321 yards, three touchdowns and no interceptions, good for a 156.1 passer rating, a number that Jared Goff matched only once.

"Getting to a new place, and being able to come out Week 1, night one, and get a win and play the way we did, feels good," said Stafford, wearing a sweater with giant yellow smiling-face emoji. "Lot of work to be done, but definitely a good start."

Stafford completed passes to Kupp, Jefferson, Robert Woods, DeSean Jackson, tight end Tyler Higbee and running back Darrell Henderson, with Kupp's seven catches for 108 yards and the touchdown leading the way. Henderson carried 16 times for 70 yards and a 1-yard touchdown dive in the third quarter.

"I think that's when we're going to be at our best," Stafford said, "when everybody gets the ball."

McVay had been trying to remind people that Jackson, the wide receiver signed last winter to add speed to the passing game, wouldn't be the team's only deep threat.

McVay demonstrated that right away when, on Stafford's third snap with the Rams, he called for Stafford to fake a handoff to Henderson, roll to the left and heave the ball back to the right to Jefferson.

Jefferson brought the ball in to his facemask at the 20-yard line, tumbled to the turf at the 15 but wasn't touched by a Chicago player and got up and outran Jaylon Johnson to the end zone.

The 67-yard catch-and-run for a touchdown was the Rams' longest pass play since a 70-yard touchdown from Goff to Kupp against the Minnesota Vikings in 2018.

Stafford strutted down the field to celebrate with Jefferson, as Rams cornerback Jalen Ramsey joined in.

"That's a debut that probably should go down in history," Ramsey said of Stafford's performance.

Cooper Kupp had a big day in the season opener with seven catches for 108 yards and a touchdown. (Los Angeles Daily News: Will Lester)

In another mark of a new year, the quarterback and the offense took the pressure off the defense instead of the other way around.

But big plays by Ramsey and the Rams' defense kept frustrating the Bears.

After the Bears used a long return of the opening kickoff and a long run by David Montgomery to get inside the Rams' 10, a pass by Andy Dalton was tipped by linebacker Kenny Young and intercepted by cornerback David Long in the end zone.

With the Bears across the 50 again on their second possession and going for it on fourth and 4, Ramsey jarred loose a pass to Allen Robinson.

Again, late in the first quarter, the Bears were in Rams territory and facing fourth and 4. Then outside linebacker Justin Hollins forced Dalton to fumble and Young recovered at the L.A. 42. Stafford to Higbee for 17 yards started a drive that stalled but resulted in Matt Gay's second field goal and a 13-0 lead.

The Bears broke through before halftime to make it 13-7.

But four plays into the second half, Stafford threw long to Kupp, who'd outrun the Bears defense. Kupp caught it just outside the 10 and went in untouched.

Stafford was touched, by defensive tackle Akiem Hicks, who drew a roughing-the-passer penalty. Stafford got up from the hit to see Kupp in the end zone. He sprinted toward the sideline with his left index finger in the air.

"I kind of rolled over and tried to get up as fast as I could to see if it was a good one," Stafford said. "I saw him trotting in the end zone. I figured it was in a good spot."

Stafford's last touchdown pass came on a two-yard play to Woods at the back of the end zone with 3:17 to play.

The pass to Jefferson is the one that will be remembered.

"I think it was a great job by him being able to flip his hips and make an unbelievable throw," McVay said of Stafford. "He's gifted. He's got a great ability to change his arm slot and make all types of throws, short, intermediate or down the field.

"You're not limited with anything you can do with him in the pass game, and hopefully we'll continue to build on the options and opportunities we have moving forward." ∎

Matthew Stafford had a memorable Rams debut, going 20 for 26 with 321 yards and three touchdowns in the romp over the Bears. (Los Angeles Daily News: Will Lester)

'THEY FINALLY CAME HOME'

LA Rams Play in Front of a SoFi Crowd for the First Time

September 12, 2021 | By Ryan Carter

Sammy Reyes stood under a popup canopy in the parking lot of Inglewood's SoFi Stadium Sunday afternoon, Sept. 12, and took stock of the party that surrounded him.

Reyes is from East L.A. But despite the miles he traveled to get there, Reyes, a lifelong Rams fan, didn't feel like a visitor.

"It's home," he said.

Reyes joined thousands of other football fans in converging on SoFi on this late summer day to celebrate the first Los Angeles Rams game of the 2021-22 NFL season.

But it was more than that.

It was, in a way, a homecoming. And a long-awaited one at that.

The regular season kick-off between the Rams and the visiting Chicago Bears marked the second campaign the Los Angeles football team has played in in SoFi, a 70,000-seat, technologically marvelous stadium years in the making. Last season, however, was played without fans because of the coronavirus pandemic.

But those fans, many of whom stuck with the franchise through relocation after relocation — LA to Anaheim to St. Louis and back to LA — finally got a chance to be with their team. And root for them in person.

And they partied. Or rather, tailgated. Hip hop and mariachi music created a cacophony. The aroma of barbecue filled the parking lot. Smartphones put in overtime taking photos of the moment.

"They finally came home," said Joe E. Hernandez, of Whittier. "It's like when you find someone you love, and then they leave but then come back. You know it was meant to be."

Sunday's game was a long time coming.

It had a direct lineage back to at least to 2013, when St. Louis Rams owner and Chairman Stan Kroenke met with Inglewood Mayor James Butts. The meeting was supposed to last 15 minutes. Instead, they huddled for two-and-a-half hours, plotting "an action plan" to make a stadium happen.

The Rams returned to Los Angeles in 2016, taking up temporary residence in their old stomping grounds, the Los Angeles Memorial Coliseum.

And plans moved forward for a $5 billion project that officials say is transforming a city that just nine years ago was on the verge of bankruptcy. SoFi, on the former Hollywood Park racetrack property not far from LAX, is part of a larger 298-acre sports and entertainment destination being developed.

The stadium normally sits about 70,000 — the Rams sold 70,455 tickets for Sunday — but can expand to 100,000. A 70,000-square-foot video board — a dual-sided techno-marvel — seems to float over the field.

The Rolling Stones play here in October.

But the stadium, as the fans would say, is the Rams' house.

As the 5:20 p.m. start time neared, fans slowly left the parking lot and went inside their new cathedral. And even those wearing the wrong colors were impressed.

"It's awesome," said John Dyer, from Chicago. He attended the game with his son and his brother, Kevin Dyer. Kevin Dyer's reaction was similar:

"Amazing."

The cheer and reverence inside and outside SoFi was

The season opening win against the Bears was the first Rams game at SoFi Stadium with fans in attendance, marking the true homecoming of the franchise back to L.A. (Los Angeles Daily News: Will Lester)

a stark difference from the surreal 2020 season.

Last year was supposed to be the Rams homecoming. And they did play in SoFi.

But county health orders designed to prevent the spread of the coronavirus kept fans away. The seats were empty, except for fan cutouts on both ends of the field. The team's first home game also opened amid historic social unrest in the nation, and in L.A., where the outcry against racism was seen on the field, with several players taking a knee during the national anthem.

The coronavirus is still around, causing some health orders — such as masking — to return.

But that didn't seem to dampen spirits.

In the parking lot, fans played catch. They drank and played games. They played drinking games. They chanted.

"Whether we're masked or not," said Palm Springs resident John White, "we're going to show up."

There was some grumbling, however.

Long lines of vehicles filled the narrow thoroughfares into the stadium's lots, with fans complaining about hour-plus-long waits on surrounding streets just get into SoFi once they arrived off local freeways. Those gameday complaints about echoed preseason rumblings over

traffic, spotty WiFi and the need for more concession offerings — something the Rams said they would work to improve.

Still, the frustration was countered with the angst of youngsters and old-timers wanting to see stars like quarterback Matthew Stafford and cornerback Darious Williams perform.

Finally, inside the packed stadium, the game got underway — and thousands cheered for the Rams.

The Rams scored early when quarterback Matthew Stafford hit Van Jefferson for a 67-yard touchdown — the Rams' longest pass completion since 2018.

Sandra Marie Ramirez said her dad, Manuel Ignacio Valle, would have been pleased.

Ramirez's father, an El Monte resident and lifelong Rams fan, died last year. So his daughter came from Las Vegas to be at Sunday's game for him.

"My heart is for my dad," she said.

As the fourth quarter wound down, the Rams had a comfortable lead. The Rams have seven more games at SoFi this season, not counting the playoffs. That's seven more chances for their fans to come home.

At last. ∎

5

CORNERBACK

JALEN RAMSEY

Rams' All-Pro CB is Getting a Corner on Versatility

September 17, 2021 | By Kevin Modesti

During his first two years with the Rams, Jalen Ramsey earned a reputation as the No. 1 lockdown cornerback in the NFL, the best at stopping an opponent from even trying to pass to its top receiver.

By the time this year is out, that superlative might seem like faint praise.

"I don't view myself as just a corner," Ramsey said Friday after the Rams (1-0) finished practice for their first road game of the season Sunday against the Indianapolis Colts (0-1).

Increasingly, the Rams and their opponents don't view Ramsey in such narrow terms either, assuming opponents can even get a useful view of a player who confuses quarterbacks by lining almost anywhere on the defensive side of the field.

This started during the 2020 season, when Ramsey began to play the versatile "star position," something that then-defensive coordinator Brandon Staley said was "like a LeBron James is used in the basketball court, where he's a positionless player."

But in 2021, Ramsey's role is a feature of the gameplan from Week 1 as new coordinator Raheem Morris looks for ways to improve on a defense that allowed the fewest points, yards and passing yards in the league.

Early in the Rams' 34-14 victory over the Chicago Bears on Sunday night at SoFi Stadium, Ramsey broke up a fourth-down pass by Andy Dalton to wide receiver Allen Robinson. Relatively routine stuff for a cornerback.

Then, in a span of four plays on the Bears' next series, Ramsey was credited with three tackles behind the line of scrimmage: a three-yard loss by running back Damien Williams on the left end, a two-yard loss on a carry by wide receiver Marquise Goodwin at the left sideline and a two-yard loss on a pass to wide receiver Darnell Mooney on the right side. Not routine for anyone, let alone a cornerback.

On a team with NFC Offensive Player of the Week Matthew Stafford at quarterback and NFL Defensive Player of the Year Aaron Donald on the line, the most watchable player might be Ramsey. The three-time All-Pro, already a star when the Rams acquired him in a 2019 trade with the Jacksonville Jaguars, has only gotten better, in more and more ways.

When websites compiled rankings of the league's cornerbacks this summer, Ramsey came in No. 1

Jalen Ramsey is accustomed to celebrating since he joined the Rams, as he's been selected to three Pro Bowls and two All-Pro teams in his tenure in L.A. (Los Angeles Daily News: Keith Birmingham)

ahead of the Ravens' Marlon Humphreys, Dolphins' Xavien Howard, Bills' Tre'Davious White, Packers' Jaire Alexander and Patriots' Stephon Gilmore.

But when Rams coach Sean McVay was asked Friday whom he would compare Ramsey to, he replied: "I think he's kind of one of one."

"It's different," Donald said of Ramsey's role, which can find him positioned up close to Donald on the line, blitzing or playing like an edge-rushing linebacker. "I was watching film and seeing him coming up in a box, hitting some linemen and holding the ends. (There isn't a) player like him in the National Football League. He can do it all."

This wouldn't work if the Rams didn't have other versatile cornerbacks, able to play where Ramsey doesn't, whether that's outside or in the slot. Troy Hill last year. Darious Williams this year.

But the key ingredient is Ramsey's size (a lanky 6-foot-1 and 208 pounds) and the fact he's more willing to hit than most cornerbacks.

"I think it's really fair to say that 'willing' is an understatement," Morris said Thursday. "This guy absolutely embraces it and loves it and wants it."

Ramsey, 26, the fifth overall pick in the 2016 draft out of Florida State, wanted to be more than a cornerback from the beginning but didn't get the chance with the Jaguars.

"Last year, it was sprinkled in here and there, but this year it's kind of no boundaries to where I may be during the game," Ramsey said Friday. "I don't know where I'm going to be playing each week when I come in here Wednesdays and try to figure out the game plan. It might change Wednesday and Thursday. I don't know. It might change on game day."

Against the Bears, Ramsey made a career-high nine tackles.

That fulfilled the coaches' goal of positioning the NFL's highest-salaried cornerback where the action is.

"He's going to get more play opportunities," McVay said, "and the more play opportunities Jalen Ramsey has, the better it is for the Rams football team." ■

Jalen Ramsey came to the Rams with a reputation as a shutdown corner and has evolved into one of the most versatile defensive backs in recent NFL history. (Los Angeles Daily News: David Crane)

Rams 27, Colts 24

September 19, 2021 • Indianapolis, Indiana

STAYING THE COURSE

Rams Overcome Mistakes, Get Late Field Goal to Beat Colts

By Kevin Modesti

The game had gone haywire. Lucas Oil Stadium was bedlam. The Rams found themselves tied with the underdog Colts late in the fourth quarter.

Matthew Stafford had 'em right where he wants 'em.

The master of fourth-quarter comebacks and game-winning drives when he was the Detroit Lions' quarterback isn't likely to need that famous poise as often with a Rams team that doesn't trail as often.

But when the Rams needed it for the first time Sunday, Stafford coolly led them to a touchdown and late field goal to come away from a rough day with a 27-24 victory over the Colts and a 2-0 start to the season.

Teammates said they felt more confident they'd pull it out because they knew they had Stafford, author of 38 game-winning drives with the Lions, the most in the NFL over the past 12 years.

"I don't know if they (were) or not," Stafford said afterward. "I was as calm as could be."

Calm was just what the Rams needed after a game they led by 11 in the third quarter started to get away from them.

First, linebacker Kenny Young was ejected for making contact with an official as he protested a decision deep in Rams territory, and three plays later two Carson Wentz passes gave the Colts a touchdown and two-point conversion and cut the Rams' lead to 17-14 late in the third quarter.

Then, an errant snap in punt formation from the 11 allowed Ashton Dulin to recover in the end zone to put the Colts ahead for the first time at 21-17 early in the fourth. Matt Orzech's snap hit Nick Scott near the line of scrimmage, and punter Johnny Hekker chased the bouncing ball but couldn't control it.

Worse, the Rams had lost starting running back Darrell Henderson to a rib injury on his first carry of the quarter.

"It was a lot. A lot of teams would fold in those circumstances," Rams coach Sean McVay said. "Our guys stayed the course.

"(Stafford) had a look in his eye. He relishes those moments. And he was at his best when his best was required."

After the Colts (0-2) kicked off leading by four with 14:12 to play, Stafford took the Rams 70 yards in four plays, hitting wide receiver Cooper Kupp for a 44-yard catch and run to the Indianapolis 10 before they connected for their second touchdown pass of the day and third of the season.

The Colts came back and tied at 24 it on a field goal with 7:22 to play.

Stafford got the ball at the 25. The winning drive

The Rams and Matthew Stafford weren't at their best against the Colts, but they made enough plays late in the game to come away with the victory. (AP Images)

wasn't all the quarterback. Sony Michel, seeing his first action of 2021 as Henderson's replacement, carried six times on the 12-play drive for 36 yards. Stafford completed three passes for 24 yards. But his calm was key.

On third down and 1 at the Rams' 48, Stafford was scrambling and was out of all options except one. He side-armed the ball to the right sideline to find Kupp (who else?). Kupp sidestepped a tackler and drove toward the first-down stick to gain the last three of his 163 receiving yards Sunday.

After a Kupp run went backward on third and 2 at the Colts' 15, McVay sent in kicker Matt Gay, whose 38-yard field goal was good.

More than two minutes remained. The crowd of 63,076 was roaring for another twist, with Jacob Eason at quarterback after a Wentz injury. But Rams cornerback Jalen Ramsey picked off an Eason pass.

It was the last big play of the day for a Rams defense that is making a habit of that.

A Leonard Floyd sack of Wentz on fourth down at the Rams' 1 stopped the Colts' first drive, and a Troy Reeder interception of a Wentz shovel pass on third down from the Rams' 3 stopped another.

Two other third-down stops, after the Colts drove to the Rams' 30 and 28, ended in field goals to make it 10-6 at halftime.

A week earlier, the Rams were in a tight game at halftime only to blow out the Bears in the second half and win 34-14.

It wasn't as clear-cut this time.

After they went up 17-6 on Henderson's two-yard touchdown early in the second half, they hit what players and coaches euphemistically refer to as adversity.

"Good time of the year to do that, to find out what we're made of," Reeder said.

Good quarterback to have at the controls, too.

"When we're in the huddle, it's not like we're thinking, 'Oh, we've got the quarterback who's led the most game-winning drives in the fourth quarter,'" Kupp said. "It's more just his demeanor, how he has control of the offense, and really just the understanding and belief we have in each other."

Stafford committed his first turnover with the Rams when a second-quarter pass intended for Kupp over the middle seemed to slip out of Stafford's hand and sailed to safety Khari Willis.

Stafford finished the day 19 for 30 for 278 yards, two touchdowns and the interception.

So the new Rams quarterback wasn't perfect, as he'd very nearly been against the Bears, but he delivered what was needed.

"I need a beer," McVay said as he walked out after his post-game press conference.

Stafford still looked as calm as could be. ■

The L.A. run defense held up their end of the bargain, limiting the potent Colts running attack to only 109 yards. (AP Images)

Rams 34, Buccaneers 24

September 26, 2021 • Inglewood, California

GET THE PARTY STARTED

Rams, Matthew Stafford Ace Test, Beat Super Bowl Champion Bucs

By Kevin Modesti

The Rams started the day under high pressure, with no less on the line than the world's judgment of whether they're contenders or pretenders and whether Matthew Stafford can take them where Tom Brady took the Tampa Bay Buccaneers.

But by the third quarter Sunday at SoFi Stadium, they were just having fun.

DeSean Jackson was prancing to a cathartic touchdown with a deep pass from Matthew Stafford, and coach Sean McVay was sprinting up the sideline to join the celebration. Kenny Young was sacking Brady, Aaron Donald was throwing a ballcarrier for a drive-ending loss, and the defense was partying. The Rams weren't just acquitting themselves against the Tampa Bay Buccaneers, they were thumping the Super Bowl champions, and the fans had SoFi rocking.

There's a lot to take away from this 34-24 Rams victory over the Bucs in front of an announced crowd of 73,205, the largest in the short history of crowds at the home of L.A.'s pro football teams.

But the lasting image is how much fun the Rams seemed to be having as the decisiveness of the win began to sink in.

"Everybody's always having fun together," Donald said of the display of camaraderie. "The last time we had a team like that, we went to the Super Bowl."

You don't always see a head coach joining in a touchdown celebration the way McVay did after Stafford hit Jackson for a 75-yard touchdown catch and run on the third play of the second half. The ball that traveled more than 60 yards in the air. It put the Rams up by two touchdowns.

"I think my hamstrings are already sore," McVay said with a laugh afterward. "It was just pure excitement. I'm not really thinking about those things in the moment, just enjoying with these guys."

Jackson, the 34-year-old Long Beach native signed last winter to provide just such a deep threat, had kept running after his first Rams touchdown into the stadium's southeast tunnel. When he came back out, he was surprised to see McVay.

"I looked up, and he was the first one there," Jackson said with a grin. "It meant a lot."

Stafford was in the next wave to greet Jackson.

"He was going crazy. Which was awesome," Stafford said of McVay. "It was a play we talked about early in the week, possibly getting D-Jack down the field on that

Matthew Stafford and the Rams got the best of defending champs Tom Brady and the Buccaneers. Stafford was spectacular in the win, throwing for 343 yards and four touchdowns. (Los Angeles Daily News: David Crane)

one. I'm glad (McVay) went to (that play) and we were able to execute."

The win made the Rams 3-0 for the third time in McVay's five years, the first of those fast starts having come in the 2018 run to the Super Bowl.

More tests await, as soon as next Sunday when the Rams host the 3-0 Arizona Cardinals in their first NFC West game of the season.

But they couldn't ace an early-season test much more than they did against Brady and the Bucs.

Stafford passed for 343 yards and four touchdowns, completing 27 of 38. Jackson caught three passes for 120 yards, including a 40-yard catch-and-run that set up Stafford's 10-yard touchdown pass to Cooper Kupp caught nine for 96 yards and his fourth and fifth touchdowns of the season. Sony Michel, subbing for injured Darrell Henderson at running back, gained tough, important yards among his 67 on 20 carries.

The defense, meanwhile, stopped the Bucs' ground game and forced Brady to pass. Brady threw for 432 yards, but the Rams kept receivers in front of them and prevented game-changing plays. An incomplete pass on fourth-and-2 at the Bucs' 48 with 7:10 to play seemed to seal the end of Tampa Bay's 10-game winning streak.

The Rams sacked Brady three times. Young's punctuated a 10-tackle day of redemption for the ex-UCLA linebacker who was ejected from last week's win over the Indianapolis Colts for bumping an official. Donald got his first-ever sack against the quarterback widely hailed as the Greatest of All Time.

The game between 2-0 teams was billed as both a measuring stick for the Rams' capability of getting to Super Bowl LVI next February at SoFi Stadium, and a quarterback duel.

The duel began quietly, and then started to crackle.

It was scoreless when Stafford got the ball at the Rams' 5 late in the first quarter and set out on a 14-play drive on which he completed all eight of his passes for 74 yards, the last six a touchdown to tight end Tyler Higbee.

Brady immediately matched Stafford. From the Bucs' 24, he took Tampa Bay on a 15-play drive, completing 8 of 9 for 73 yards before wide receiver Chris Godwin ran two yards for the touchdown.

Stafford came right back down the field, going 6 for 8 for 67 yards on a 75-yard drive capped by a 2-yard pass to Kupp in the end zone with 51 seconds to play in the half.

Stafford was rolling now, on his way to leading the Rams to four straight touchdown drives, plus the short drive to a 48-yard Matt Gay field goal that made it a three-score game for the first time at 31-14 late in the third quarter.

Among those enjoying watching Stafford was Donald.

"I seen him outside the (locker-room) door and I gave him a big hug and said, 'I love you, man,'" Donald said.

"Those hugs are a lot better than the old ones," said Stafford, remembering when he was with the Detroit Lions, being chased by Donald.

Stafford does something new each game, and this time it was finally connecting deep to Jackson, who'd been little used in Weeks 1 and 2. Stafford missed Jackson on their first two tries Sunday. Then came the Rams' longest pass play since 2017.

Said Jackson: "(I'm) just trying to figure out a role, and just being patient. Me and Sean had a long conversation, and (he said), 'Be patient, I'm going to figure out how to get you the ball.'"

When he did, Sunday's party started. ■

Running back Sony Michel (25) ran for 67 tough yards on 20 carries in the victory. (Los Angeles Daily News: David Crane)

Rams 26, Seahawks 17

October 7, 2021 • Seattle, Washington

UNFAZED

Robert Woods Helps Rams Bounce Back to Beat Seahawks

By Kevin Modesti

For a while there, it was looking like a fast fall for the Rams, in danger of a second loss in five days that would have left a team with early-season Super Bowl hype instead looking at the title of September Bowl champions.

But they caught themselves Thursday night at Lumen Field, using their knack for shaking off slow starts to come from behind and beat the Seattle Seahawks, 26-17.

Robert Woods did most of the catching.

The wide receiver, a missing man for much of the Rams' first loss of the season against the Arizona Cardinals on Sunday, caught 12 passes for 150 yards, close to his career highs, to lead the offense's revival.

"Nobody was fazed by the loss last week," Woods said. "Being able to come back against a division opponent like this, in Seattle, get a win on a short week, the guys are just poised."

He was the big target as quarterback Matthew Stafford had his highest-yardage game as a Ram, completing 25 of 37 passes for 365 yards and one touchdown, despite one bad interception early on.

Stafford did that despite banging the index finger on his throwing hand in the second quarter and being looked at by trainers on the sideline.

"It didn't affect me too much, to be honest with you," Stafford said of the finger, but he said he had to pop the joint back into place and wore a bandage on it after the game.

The defense, meanwhile, recovered from a bad day against the Cardinals' Kyler Murray to contain Seahawks dual-threat Russell Wilson before the quarterback left the game in the second half with his own finger injury.

The Rams had two takeaways and had two sacks of Wilson, one of them by Aaron Donald, giving the defensive tackle 88½ in his career, breaking a tie with Leonard Little for the franchise record in the era since sacks became an official statistic.

The Rams are 4-1 and smiling as they did after the win over the Tampa Bay Buccaneers that made them 3-0 in September and the darlings of Super Bowl futures bettors.

The Seahawks fell to 2-3.

The Rams took their first lead of the game on their first drive of the second half, going 96 yards after a punt, 68 on a catch and run by DeSean Jackson on a Stafford pass that seemed underthrown, and the last 5 on a carry by Darrell Henderson. Matt Gay missed an extra-point attempt for the first time this season, and it was 9-7.

Then they made it back-to-back touchdown drives, going 82 yards after another punt, with a pair of 20-yard completions from Stafford to Woods and a 29-yard run by Henderson to set up a 13-yard pass to Tyler Higbee

Robert Woods was unstoppable in the win over the Seahawks, hauling in 12 catches for 150 yards. (AP Images)

in the end zone. It was a two-score lead, 16-7, late in the third quarter.

The Rams seemed to be in even better shape when Wilson had to leave the game after dislocating a finger on his throwing hand. But Geno Smith came in and led a 98-yard drive, the last 23 on a pass to D.K. Metcalf, cutting the lead to two points early in the fourth.

Stafford responded, completing passes for 24 yards to Woods and 33 and 13 to Cooper Kupp before Sony Michel ran 2 yards untouched to make it 23-14 with 6:08 left.

It wasn't a fourth-quarter comeback, something the Rams' new quarterback is famous for, but coolly leading a 73-yard drive with a nervous lead was pure Stafford.

"Just like Indy, when we went behind," said Rams coach Sean McVay, recalling Stafford's game-winning drive against the Indianapolis Colts in Week 2. "You keep getting the ball in his hands, and he makes plays.

"He made a bunch of timely throws right there. You see when we're firing on all cylinders, we can be explosive. We've got to do it more consistently, but there was a lot of things we can take from that."

A Seahawks field goal kept the game alive with 2:45 on the clock.

After the Rams couldn't run out said clock, it was up to the defense. And that unit came through with the big play that had been elusive lately. Nick Scott intercepted a Smith pass at the Seattle 32 with 2:02 left, and a 47-yard field goal by Matt Gay with 1:24 to go sealed the win.

The teams came into their first meeting since the Rams' playoff game in Seattle last January – and their fourth meeting in 11 months – both needing to win to avoid falling farther behind the NFC West-leading Cardinals.

In the first half, the two star-studded offenses, operating against struggling defenses, produced enough mistakes to gladden viewers in Arizona.

The Seahawks led 7-3 thanks to a 19-yard touchdown pass from Wilson to Metcalf in the second quarter,

capping a quick 83-yard drive on which the big play was a pass interference call.

That 47-yard penalty was committed by Robert Rochell, the rookie replacing David Long at nickel cornerback, who was being outrun by Metcalf on a deep throw.

Both teams lost chances for more.

Stafford threw an interception to safety Quandre Diggs in the end zone when he was trying to throw it away on second and goal at the 8.

"I've just got to throw it away away," Stafford said.

Wilson seemed to have cashed in a Seahawks drive to the Rams' 15, but his completion to Tyler Lockett in the end zone was wiped out by a Seattle holding penalty. The Seahawks tried to settle for a field goal but missed.

The Rams have done this a few times already this season, starting slow on offense and then igniting. Usually, Stafford's main target has been Kupp, leading some to wonder what happened to Woods. But Thursday, the Serra High (Gardena) and USC product was getting open and back in the prime-time spotlight.

Targeted just twice in the first half of the Cardinals game, Woods was thrown to six times and caught all six passes for 67 yards in the first half Thursday. Then he stepped up his production in the second half.

He said he had initiated a conversation with McVay to say, "give me some targets."

"Just being a competitor, just trying to do everything, being a part of helping this team win," Woods said. "(I got) an opportunity to get my number called and have some plays and capitalize on those opportunities."

Apparently, the conversation went well.

"He deserved it. We were definitely trying to get him the ball," McVay said. "He's a stud, and I just loved the way he was instrumental in the win tonight." ■

Offensive guard Austin Corbett (63) and the Rams offensive line helped L.A. bounce back from a loss to the Cardinals in Week 4. (AP Images)

Rams 38, Giants 11

October 17, 2021 • East Rutherford, New Jersey

REVVING THE ENGINE

Rams Overcome Slow Start to Rout Giants

By Kevin Modesti

It takes a couple of turns of the ignition key sometimes, but when the Rams' offense gets started, it fires on as many cylinders as any in the NFL.

Add head-starts from the defense, and it's hard to keep up with.

In what became a 38-11 victory over the New York Giants at MetLife Stadium on Sunday, the Rams began sluggishly before roaring to life, led by Matthew Stafford and, well, almost everyone else in blue and yellow.

Coach Sean McVay couldn't help thinking about the frustration of the first quarter, when third-down sacks ended both of the Rams' possessions.

"I thought we could be a lot sharper offensively," McVay said. "We've got to start faster. There's no excuse. We've got to be better than that. But we'll take the win, and I thought guys did a nice job."

When the offense got going, it quickly showed what McVay wishes it could be from the first snap.

But you might put it the other way, that the cold start made the eventual combustion all the more impressive.

After punts ended the first two possessions, and back-to-back penalties to begin the third put the Rams in first and 21, the switch was flipped.

Five consecutive big gains, with five different players getting the ball, showed the difference in class between Sunday's teams.

Running back Darrell Henderson ripped off a nine-yard gain. Stafford hit wide receiver Cooper Kupp up the right sideline for 28 yards into Giants territory. Stafford connected with tight end Tyler Higbee on the left side for 10. Back on the ground, running back Sony Michel ran over a tackler at the end of a 15-yard charge. To cap it off, wide receiver Robert Woods got open over the middle, caught Stafford's pass at the 10, spun right and scored untouched.

A New York crowd that had been excited by the Giants' 14-play opening drive and 3-0 lead fell silent and would stay that way on a sunny but crisp afternoon, until Eli Penny's short run put the home team in the end zone for the first time with 6:21 to play.

The victory made the Rams 5-1, including 3-0 on the road. The Giants fell to 1-5.

After much-anticipated games against the Buccaneers (a win), Cardinals (loss) and Seahawks (win), the Rams faced the question of whether they could maintain their intensity in a run of games against the Giants, Lions and Texans, beginning with a 10 a.m. L.A. time kickoff Sunday.

Under those circumstances, a 27-point win was nothing to complain about.

"I think it's just not listening to outside noise," safety Taylor Rapp said of fighting off a letdown. "It's about

Running back Darrell Henderson had 107 yards from scrimmage and two touchdowns in the big win over the Giants. (AP Images)

taking care of our business and just playing our ball."

The Rams would score on four of their five possessions in the second quarter and their first two in the second half, thanks in no small part to two interceptions by Rapp and one by cornerback Robert Rochell.

Stafford completed 22 of 28 passes for 251 yards, four touchdowns and one interception, while being sacked more than once in a game for the first time this year, before going to the sideline for safety early in the fourth quarter and letting John Wolford see his first action of the season.

Kupp had nine receptions for 130 yards and his sixth and seventh touchdowns of the season. Henderson ground out 78 yards and a touchdown on 21 carries. Henderson caught a scoring pass too.

Two of those touchdowns, Kupp's first and Henderson's, were set up by big plays by a defense that had its splashiest game of the season, even if it did come against a Giants offense that began without injured running back Saquon Barkley and receiver Kenny Golladay and lost receiver Kadarius Toney early.

A strip sack of Giants quarterback Daniel Jones by Ogbonnia Okoronkwo, and fumble recovery by Leonard Floyd, set up a three-yard sidearm touchdown pass from Stafford to Kupp just inside the right goal-line pylon to make it 14-3 in the second quarter.

Rapp's first interception gave the Rams the ball deep in Giants territory again, and Henderson went over from two yards out to make it 21-3.

Henderson scored again on the next series, hauling in a 25-yard pass from Stafford at the goal line, and it had become a rout before halftime.

At that point, though, the Rams were only one for five in converting third downs, and there had been penalties and sacks against what had been the league's least-penalized and least sacked-team.

"I don't want to continue to come up here and continue to say the same things," said McVay, who has seen the offense start slowly repeatedly. "We've got to do a better job. I've got to do a better job. It was a great job by our defense putting us in position to be able to score points as a team."

After giving up chunks of yardage on the Giants' first possession, with Rochell burned twice by Toney, the secondary did well in the first of at least three games it will need Terrell Burgess, David Long and Donte Deayon to make up for the absence of injured cornerback Darious Williams.

"I thought they did a hell of a job today, like they've been doing all season," Stafford said of the defense. "We didn't start as fast as we wanted to, and they kept us right there in it.

"They know once we hit the ground running, we're tough to stop."

It says something about the Rams' expectations, Kupp said, that a team can win 38-11 and think it can improve.

"It does speak to the standard we have as a team and an offense and what we're supposed to do," Kupp said. "This is the result we wanted, but as an offense it's not up to our standard in terms of the process of how we execute as a unit.

"We've got the right guys. We have all the right guys that know we can be better." ∎

Quarterback Daniel Jones had little room to operate all day, as the Rams defense sacked him four times and forced him into three interceptions. (AP Images)

Rams 28, Lions 19
October 24, 2021 • Inglewood, California

STAFFORD WINS QB FACEOFF

Rams Top Old Friend Goff, Lions in Battle of Traded Signal Callers

By Tribune News Service

Jared Goff returned to SoFi Stadium with the Detroit Lions with a chance to live down the perception that Matthew Stafford and the Rams won their blockbuster trade last winter.

Stafford and the Rams won the game too.

In a story arc familiar to followers of Goff's career in L.A., he had a great start but a sad finish, allowing the Rams to come from 10 points behind to win 28-19 in front of 70,540 fans at SoFi Stadium.

Goff, who had many good moments in L.A., added another one on the Lions' first possession by connecting on a short pass that running back D'Andre Swift turned into a 63-yard touchdown.

Stafford, who spent 12 personally prolific but ultimately frustrating years in Detroit, brought the Rams back to take the lead on a 5-yard touchdown pass to Cooper Kupp with 13:59 to play.

The Lions' chance of winning effectively ended when Goff was hit by Aaron Donald as he threw a pass into the end zone and it was intercepted by Jalen Ramsey with less than five minutes on the clock.

Matt Gay added a 47-yard field goal with 58 seconds left to secure the Rams' win.

Stafford finished with 28 completions on 41 attempts for 334 yards, three touchdowns and no interceptions.

Goff went 22 for 36 for 268 yards, one TD and two interceptions.

Kupp caught 10 passes for 156 yards and his seventh and eighth touchdowns of the season.

The Rams are 6-1. The Lions are 0-7.

The duel between Stafford and Goff started out more like a duel between Rams coach Sean McVay and Lions coach Dan Campbell, with Campbell rewarded for aggressiveness.

After the opening touchdown, the Lions tried an onside kick — and recovered it at their 47. On fourth and 7 from the 50, they faked a punt — and punter Jack Fox threw to Bobby Price for 17 yards.

That drive resulted in a 37-yard field goal by Austin Seibert and a 10-0 lead for the Lions midway through the first quarter.

That's as good as it got for the considerable number of fans in Lions jerseys in the SoFi Stadium crowd.

Two defensive penalties helped the Rams convert third downs on an 11-play, 84-yard drive to a touchdown on Stafford's 11-yard pass to Van Jefferson behind Jerry Jacobs at the left edge of the end zone. The Rams were within 13-10.

Goff began the Lions' next possession by throwing a pass to an ineligible receiver and then dumping one

Matthew Stafford was sharp in victory once again, throwing for 334 yards and three touchdowns against his former team. [Los Angeles Daily News: Will Lester]

at the feet of an eligible one. The Lions' first punt of the day gave the Rams a chance to go in front before halftime. Again, Stafford cashed it in.

A 2-yard pass play from Stafford to Cooper Kupp for the wide receiver's seventh touchdown of the season gave the Rams what became a 17-16 lead at the break.

It was the first time Goff and Stafford, traded for each other in January, faced their former teams.

The Rams showed videos of highlights of Goff's and Lions defensive end Michael Brockers' careers in L.A. With all eyes on them, Goff and Rams coach Sean McVay got nowhere close to a handshake during warmups, but McVay embraced Goff at game's end. Goff and Stafford served as captains for the coin flip and exchanged a quick hug.

Stafford won the coin flip too. ■

Opposite and Above: Cooper Kupp continued his torrid start to the season, torching the Lions for 10 catches for 156 yards and two touchdowns. (Los Angeles Daily News: Will Lester)

Rams 38, Texans 22

October 31, 2021 • Houston, Texas

STAY THE COURSE

Unfazed by Off-Field Distractions, Rams Wallop Texans for Fourth Win in a Row

By Kevin Modesti

It was a weird week by the standards of the usually well-oiled Rams, with one prominent player traded, another seeking to be traded, and some starters injured. It might be a wild week ahead, with more action expected around the NFL trade deadline.

In between, the Rams enjoyed a relatively drama-free 38-22 victory over the Houston Texans at NRG Stadium.

If they wanted peace and quiet, they got it. The home team left it until late in the game to offer reasons to cheer for a crowd that was socially distanced, but not for health reasons. Houston sports fans had better things to shout about, with the Astros in the World Series.

Wide receiver Robert Woods, whose second touchdown made it 38-0 in the fourth quarter before the Rams pulled most of their starters, said players had to "stay the course" amid the distractions of the trade of linebacker Kenny Young and the imminent parting with wide receiver DeSean Jackson.

"We've got a game to play," Woods said. "It was guys trying to get in a rhythm, stay locked in and get this win. Off-the-field stuff, we've just got to let it go when we get between those lines."

Before pulling most of their starters in the fourth quarter, the Rams rolled up big numbers on offense and had a shutout on defense until the Texans scored three times against the backups in the last nine minutes.

"I really liked how we came out from the jump," Rams coach Sean McVay said, "to be able to come out on the opening drive to score, get the stop and then be able to go right back down the field."

Cooper Kupp, coming into the game leading the league with 56 receptions, 809 yards and nine touchdowns, recorded another seven catches for 115 yards and one touchdown, an 11-yard pass from Matthew Stafford that made it 31-0 in the third quarter.

Darrell Henderson rushed for a season-high 90 yards, carrying for one touchdown and catching a Stafford pass for another, running behind a line that had a good day with Joe Noteboom filling in at left tackle for injured Andrew Whitworth.

Stafford completed 21 of 32 passes for 305 yards and three touchdowns, giving him 22 touchdown passes in eight games for the Rams, more than Jared Goff had all last season.

After 12 seasons with the Detroit Lions, Stafford is enjoying his first experience on a team that's 7-1 at what used to be the midpoint of an NFL schedule, before this year's expansion to 17 games.

The Rams are 7-1 (the Texans fell to 1-7) and pulled into a first-place tie in the NFC West on wins and losses,

Matthew Stafford continued his stellar play as a member of the Rams, passing for 305 yards and three touchdowns. (AP Images)

though the 7-1 Arizona Cardinals officially lead the division based on the head-to-head tiebreaker, having won the teams' first meeting.

"I feel lucky to be where I am, surrounded by the people I'm surrounded by," Stafford said. "Every week, you've got to go out there and prove it."

Kupp's first three catches and 37 yards came on the Rams' opening drive to a 3-yard touchdown pass from Stafford to Henderson.

Stafford threw his second touchdown pass of the game when he hit Woods from 2 yards out after Ernest Jones' interception in the second quarter.

Woods later ran 16 yards with a Stafford pitchout for the touchdown that made it 38-0 with :02 to go in the third quarter.

Things will get harder for the Rams, who face the Tennessee Titans and road games against the San Francisco 49ers and Green Bay Packers in November.

Sunday, the Rams were completing a stretch of three games — and wins — against the soft-touch New York Giants, Lions and Texans (now 1-7).

But it hadn't been as easy a week as it should have been.

Players were caught off guard when the Rams announced last Monday morning they were trading Young to the Denver Broncos in a deal involving draft picks and the benefit of salary-cap relief.

Then, on Friday, coach Sean McVay confirmed the Rams agreed to let Jackson seek a new team after he saw less and less action since a 75-yard touchdown in Week 3 against the Tampa Bay Buccaneers.

With more cap room to play with and Jackson to trade or potentially release, the Rams will have activity of some kind before the NFL's trade deadline Tuesday at 1 p.m. Los Angeles time.

Jackson didn't travel with the team to Houston. Pregame scratches included Whitworth (knee) and nose tackle Sebastian Joseph-Day (pec), both injured in last week's victory over the Lions. Cornerback Robert Rochell (knee) didn't get on the field Sunday, though

McVay said he was available if needed.

Jones, the rookie drafted in the third round from South Carolina, made his first NFL start in Young's spot and made the afternoon's big defensive play. Stepping in front of Danny Amendola at the Texans' left sideline, Jones intercepted fellow rookie Davis Mills' pass, kept his balance and stayed in bounds, and returned it to the Houston 12. That set up the first Woods touchdown.

"It was kind of everything I've been wanting," Jones said of getting his chance to play. "I come into every game and I want to affect it in any way — tackles, breakups, anything."

Jones filled the stat sheet, finishing with a team-high seven tackles, a share of a sack, another tackle for loss and two hits on the quarterback, although he negated a big play when his illegal-hands-to-the-face penalty wiped out Donte Deayon's first NFL interception.

"Ernest Jones balled out," said defensive tackle Greg Gaines, who played more with Joseph-Day out and recorded a half-sack.

The defense, seeking the Rams' first shutout since a 34-0 win over the Cardinals in 2018, was teeing off on Mills and one of the NFL's worst offenses in the third quarter.

Leonard Floyd was credited with 2-1/2 sacks and one solo sack in a span of two three-and-out possessions for the Texans in the third quarter, giving him 6-1/2 for the season. Aaron Donald had two, his first multi-sack game this season, and has 5-1/2.

McVay didn't sound bothered by the backup defense giving up three touchdowns and a two-point conversion in the fourth quarter, a futile rally to within 16 by the Texans that made a difference for bettors on either side of a 16-1/2-point spread.

"I thought they were really smothering," McVay said of the first-unit defense. "I know we see those points on the board at the end, but when you look at the guys that are our starters and our first groups, I thought they did a great job applying pressure."

The Rams' special teams had the game's last word

Darrell Henderson (27) had a strong day against the Texans, rushing for 90 yards and a touchdown, and adding another receiving touchdown. (AP Images)

when Ben Skowronek downed a Johnny Hekker punt at the Texans' 2 with 1:51 on the clock.

But special teams had more bad moments, giving up an onside kick during the Texans' late-game rally and a 44-yard kickoff return in the first half, and seeing punt returner Tutu Atwell knocked out of the game with a shoulder injury early in the second half.

McVay said he didn't have an immediate update on Atwell's status.

Atwell, the slightly built second-round draft pick, has been mentioned as an option to replace Jackson

as the Rams' nominal big-play receiver. But the rest of their receivers continued to show they can team up with Stafford to produce explosive gains. Van Jefferson beat the Texans' defense for a 68-yard catch and run to set up Kupp's touchdown.

"We're not worried about it. You guys are talking about it," Woods said. "When you look at our receiving room, we have top explosive plays week in and week out and year after year."

Different kind of week. Same kind of result. ∎

TRADE FOR VON MILLER? IT'S AN L.A. TREND

Teams Are Willing to Make the Big Move in a Way They Weren't Before, Which Is What Market Deserves

November 2, 2021 | By Jim Alexander

When Rams general manager Les Snead completed his big offseason trade of quarterbacks and brought Matthew Stafford from Detroit to L.A., we assumed he and his team were going for it. ("It," of course, meaning a berth in the Super Bowl that will be played in their home stadium this coming Feb. 13.)

Little did we suspect that there's still another level of "all in."

The Rams' acquisition of three-time All-Pro linebacker and former Super Bowl MVP Von Miller ups the ante and the expectations. It is also entirely in line with the current operating philosophy in Los Angeles sports, and if you are a fan in this town that's an overwhelmingly positive development (unless, of course, you obsess over draft picks and prospects and potential).

Granted, big deals don't always guarantee you passage to the promised land. If they did, the National League's portion of the 2021 World Series would have been played in Los Angeles instead of Atlanta, and maybe Max Scherzer and Trea Turner would have been in the lead car of the parade down Broadway after it was over. And we still have a long season to go before we can determine if the Lakers' swap for Russell Westbrook, as well as the acquisitions of Carmelo Anthony, DeAndre Jordan, et. al., will put the 17-time champs in legitimate position for No. 18.

But meekness is seldom rewarded, and pushing the chips to the center of the table when appropriate is how you should operate in North America's most diverse sports market. That's what the Rams have done with this deal, which sends 2022 second- and third-round picks to Denver while the Broncos retain responsibility for most of Miller's 2021 salary.

Miller is 32, he's in his 10th year in the NFL, and he is the active career sacks leader (110½) and 23rd all-time. His sack totals went from 14½ in 2018 to eight in 2019, he spent 2020 on injured reserve and he's at 4½ through seven games this year. He sat out the Broncos' victory over Washington on Sunday with an ankle injury and will have to pass a Rams physical when he gets to town.

But he is also going to be joining a defense that features six-time All-Pro and three-time AP Defensive Player of the Year Aaron Donald, and fellow outside linebacker Leonard Floyd, who has taken advantage of opponents' preoccupation with Donald to register 10½ sacks and 31 solo tackles last season and 6½ sacks and 17 solo tackles in 2021. And let's not forget two-time All-Pro Jalen Ramsey, whose position is unofficially (but appropriately) called "Star."

Now, just who are you going to double-team?

The Rams' defense was statistically the NFL's best last year, tops in total yards allowed (281.9), points

The Rams continued the aggressive player personnel approach with the big midseason addition of Von Miller. (AP Images)

allowed (18.5 ppg) and passing yards allowed (190.68) and third against the run (91.25). Through Week 8 this season, they're 21st overall (367.5), 21st against the pass (264.1), 11th against the run (103.4) and 10th in scoring defense (21 ppg).

Their turnover ratio is fifth this year (plus-6) compared to tied for 21st last year (minus-3), though that might have more to do with Stafford-for-Jared Goff as it does anything the defense was or wasn't doing a year ago.

But in a division where Arizona's Kyler Murray has replaced Seattle's Russell Wilson as the quarterback X-factor on the team that is the Rams' biggest threat … well, the more influencers you have on defense, the better the chance somebody will make a play. And it's safe to assume that the presence of Donald and Floyd and Ramsey will only enhance Miller, motivated among other things by free agency after this season.

That helps explain the trade in football terms. The other context: Do you suspect the Rams, still six years into rebuilding their fan base after L.A. repossessed them from St. Louis, are not just highly motivated but desperate to be a participant in that hometown Super Bowl? The opportunity certainly exists at 7-1, and to not exhaust every option to get there would be a sin.

"You're not fearing failure," Rams coach Sean McVay said Monday. "When you do stuff like that, that's followed by expectations. But we have expectations in-house. … I think it's a real credit to those guys. I think it's a real credit to Mr. (Stan) Kroenke for being able to allow us to make these moves. And that makes you feel good and that makes you want to work that much harder to try to just make these decisions right.

"Certainly, I'll be the first to tell you guys that I haven't always been right on some of the things that we've done, but you try to be more right than you are

wrong. And usually when you have good players like we're acquiring, you just get the hell out of their way."

Under these circumstances, it is easy to forget there was a time when Los Angeles fans weren't treated to such effort from their teams' executives, with some exceptions (the Jerry Buss-era Lakers leap to mind). More often, SoCal teams drafted, developed, hoped for the best but operated conservatively, hesitant to make that bold, expensive move. Fans groused but still showed up.

Maybe it was Frank McCourt's stewardship (?!) of the Dodgers from 2004-11 that opened the patrons' eyes. As later confirmed in divorce court documents, the ambition was to depress payroll (all the while as ownership looted the team) on the assumption that just winning division titles would be satisfactory. McCourt's bankruptcy ended that charade, and since then fans of local franchises have been nowhere near as willing to settle.

That's why Mookie Betts is a Dodger. It's why LeBron James and Anthony Davis and Westbrook are Lakers, why Kawhi Leonard and Paul George are Clippers … and why Ramsey, Stafford and now Miller are Rams. Those executives value winning as much as the fans do.

It's a welcome change. ∎

Making bold moves like trading for Von Miller have been a staple in the recent L.A. sports landscape and it has paid off with multiple championships across sports. [AP Images]

Rams 37, Jaguars 7
December 5, 2021 • Inglewood, California

RAMS BOUNCE BACK

L.A. Survives Sloppy First Half, Stafford Injury Scare to Top Jaguars

By Kevin Modesti

Matthew Stafford was down on his back, not far from the penalty flag drawn by one of the two big defensive lineman who'd landed on Stafford's chest after he released a pass. The Rams' quarterback was going through more pain. SoFi Stadium held its breath as trainers sprinted onto the field.

Stafford had been under fire after a series of costly mistakes in recent games, but suddenly fans faced the chilling thought of where the Rams would be without him.

He would be able to get up, walk off the field and return after missing only one play, and then keep proving his value in more enjoyable ways.

With Stafford getting off the turf to have his best game in a month, the Rams pulled away from the Jacksonville Jaguars to win 37-7 at SoFi Stadium and end a losing streak at three games.

"He's our guy. We go as he goes," Rams coach Sean McVay said after Stafford went for 26 completions in 38 attempts for 295 yards, three touchdowns and his first turnover-free game since October.

One of those completions, to wide receiver Van Jefferson for 19 yards to the Jaguars' 27 when it was still a one-score game, came on Stafford's first play back from the hit that apparently knocked the breath out of him.

"To be able to come back after that shot he took, deliver a great throw to Van over the middle and put us in scoring position, I think continues to personify the toughness and everything that's right about Matthew," McVay said.

"He's a tough guy. He won't tell me anything. 'I'm good, I'm good.' 'What's wrong with you?' 'I'm good.' "

The Rams' most lopsided victory since their 2018 Super Bowl season wasn't a perfect performance and didn't necessarily mean they've turned things around.

The Rams (8-4) asserted their superiority over the Jaguars (2-10) only after a sloppy first-half performance that gave hope to one of the NFL's worst teams.

And the celebration won't be long before the Rams go to Arizona to face the Cardinals next Monday night, with their slim chance for a division title at risk.

Their offense will have to pick up where it left off in the second half, when Stafford and Cooper Kupp began to click as they had early in the season. Stafford hit the receiver for 43 yards and then 29 and a touchdown on one drive, 8 and 19 on another drive to a short scoring pass to Van Jefferson.

After a 1-yard scoring pass to Odell Beckham Jr., the

The Rams and Matthew Stafford put an end to a three-game losing streak with the win over the Jaguars, and featured Stafford's first turnover-free game since October. (Los Angeles Daily News: Keith Birmingham)

Rams had touchdowns on their first three drives after halftime and Stafford was on his way to his best day in more than a month.

Stafford's most important accomplishment was getting through the game without an interception or fumble after throwing a pick-six and committing two turnovers in each of the Rams' losses to the Titans, 49ers and Packers in November.

"I just try to attack each game and treat it as an opportunity to go play great," Stafford said. "Sometimes that doesn't happen.

"I tried to make sure I wasn't putting the ball in harm's way, and our guys were getting open and making catches."

Kupp caught eight passes for 129 yards, reaching 100 catches in a season for the first time, maintaining his NFL leads in the major receiving categories and becoming the sixth player in the Super Bowl era to record at least 90 receiving yards in eight or more consecutive games.

With Darrell Henderson active but not playing because of a thigh injury, Sony Michel got all the carries and rushed for 121 yards and a touchdown, the best day by a Rams running back this season.

Helping was McVay's move to bolster the run blocking, repeatedly putting backup lineman Joe Noteboom in as an eligible receiver. The line fought through a hard day when center Brian Allen went out with a knee injury and left guard David Edwards with a foot injury. Coleman Shelton replaced Allen, and Edwards returned to the game.

On defense, meanwhile, Aaron Donald and Ernest Jones combined for two sacks of Jaguars quarterback Trevor Lawrence twice as the No. 1 overall draft was held to 145 yards passing.

The improved pass rush was a natural result of the Rams playing with an early lead for a change.

"It was fun," Donald said. "You got to pin your ears back a little bit."

The Rams weren't as convincing in the first half, taking one of the uglier 16-7 leads they'll ever wish to have.

Their touchdown, on a 27-yard drive to a 5-yard push by Michel, was set up by a Jaguars fumble forced by Aaron Donald and Jalen Ramsey.

But they had gone 0 for 6 on third downs — that number improved to 5 for 6 in the second half — and failed to take full advantage of their best field advantage in weeks.

They'd settled for three Matt Gay field goals, the first after starting the game in Jaguars territory thanks to first-time kickoff returner Brandon Powell's 65-yard run with the opening kick.

The Jaguars' touchdown, a 1-yard run by Carlos Hyde that cut the Rams' lead to 10-7, was the result of lax and undisciplined defense.

The Rams gave up conversions on two third downs and a fourth, a pair of those coming on runs by Lawrence. Ramsey was flagged for taunting and Darious Williams was called for holding inside the red zone. Those were two of the team's five penalties in the first half.

None of which looked worse than when Stafford was buried by the Jaguars' Roy Robertson-Harris and Dawuane Smoot as he threw a first-down pass from the Rams' 36 late in the first half. Stafford clutched his chest as he lay on the turf. John Wolford trotted out to play quarterback.

But after Wolford executed a handoff to Michel, Stafford returned from the bench and finished the field-goal drive.

"Didn't feel great," Stafford said. "I was able to kind of walk it off and keep playing. Just a little chest shot."

Stafford's health has been a topic of speculation after he missed practice time with a stiff back before the Rams' loss to the Titans, played with a sore ankle against the 49ers, and was reported to have a sore arm too.

The Rams need him to hang tough. But that goes for all of them as they stand two games behind the Cardinals in the NFC West, their division-title hopes in the balance as they go to face the division leaders in a week in Glendale, Ariz.

"It sure feels good to be back on the winning side of things," McVay said, "and now we've got to be able to build on it." ■

In just his third game with the Rams, Odell Beckham Jr. caught his second touchdown from Matthew Stafford after catching zero in six games for the Browns. (Los Angeles Daily News: Keith Birmingham)

Rams 30, Cardinals 23
December 13, 2021 • Glendale, Arizona

STEPPING UP

Depleted Rams Overcome Loss of Five Players to Covid-19 Protocols to Keep NFC West Race Alive

By Kevin Modesti

The Rams' game against the Arizona Cardinals on Monday night was always going to be a test of their place in the playoff pecking order. But in the hours before kickoff, it became something more. A test of their resources, resourcefulness and resolve.

Taking the field at State Farm Stadium without five important players lost to the COVID-19 reserve list, the Rams got big games from Matthew Stafford and Cooper Kupp on offense and Aaron Donald and Leonard Floyd on defense — and a cast of understudies all over the field.

The Rams beat the Cardinals, 30-23, to silence a red-clad crowd that wanted to cheer the home team closer to an NFC West division title.

"This was the sign of a mentally tough team," said Rams coach Sean McVay, who had to juggle lineups and game plans several times between Friday and Monday. "I'm really proud of these guys."

The win by the Rams (9-4) — their most notable victory since a September home win against Tampa Bay — cut Arizona's (10-3) lead to one game and gave them a chance at the division title with four games left in the regular season, while also solidifying their position at the top of the conference wild-card race.

Stafford passed for 287 yards and three touchdowns, without an interception. Kupp caught a career-high 13 of Stafford's 23 completions for 123 yards and a touchdown. Arizona's Kyler Murray was intercepted twice, sacked a season-worst four times and held without a scoring pass.

Stafford said it was tough hearing Monday morning that the Rams would be without two more of their best players as All-Pro cornerback Jalen Ramsey and starting tight end Tyler Higbee went on the COVID-19 reserve list.

"Sometimes when your back's against the wall, you've got less guys than you thought you were going to have going into a game, it brings us together a little bit," Stafford said.

Tied at halftime, in danger of wearing down as the undermanned team, the Rams instead came out and got touchdown passes from Stafford on their first two series of the third quarter, helped by the defense's second takeaway of the night.

A 52-yard strike to Van Jefferson at the goal line came one play after the Rams benefited from an unnecessary roughness penalty following a catch by Kupp.

After Floyd continued an inspired performance by intercepting a Murray pass, the Rams took over at the

Cooper Kupp couldn't be contained by the Cardinals, catching a career-high 13 passes for 123 yards and a touchdown. [AP Images]

Cardinals' 19-yard line and went up, 27-13, when Kupp went down and caught a 4-yard laser of a pass inside the right end-zone pylon.

The Cardinals got one of the scores back on James Conner's second touchdown run.

But Matt Gay's third field goal of the night, and 18th consecutive successful field-goal attempt, made it a two-score game again with 7:20 left.

As the season has progressed, the Rams have been confronted more and more by injuries, none bigger than wide receiver Robert Woods' season-ending knee injury.

But they had been unscathed by COVID-19 going into this week. Then, Friday, Rams leading rusher Darrell Henderson went on the list for players who test positive or have close contact with someone who did. And Saturday, right tackle Rob Havenstein and cornerback Dont'e Deayon were placed on the list.

The body blow came Monday afternoon when the Rams announced that Ramsey and Higbee were going on the COVID-19 list too.

Asked what his reaction to the Ramsey and Higbee news was, McVay said: "My initial reaction was, 'You gotta be (kidding) me.'"

That left the Rams without four starters because of coronavirus protocols, in addition to injured starting center Brian Allen.

Tight end Kendall Blanton, tackle Bobby Evans, and defensive backs David Long and Kareem Orr were among the Rams stepping into bigger roles.

If the team's confidence was frayed, they began to stitch it together as the first half proceeded.

The Cardinals, seeking to repeat their 37-20 victory at SoFi Stadium in October, had scored first on a nine-play drive to a field goal. The Rams went three and out on their first series, and they were about to fall behind 10-0 when Arizona made another sustained drive inside their 10.

Murray targeted tight end Zach Ertz in the end zone, but Donald got a hand on the pass, and linebacker Ernest Jones intercepted it near the goal line.

From the sideline, it felt like a moment of magic to Stafford, who had been talking with Rams offensive coordinator Kevin O'Connell about what the offense would do if the Cardinals scored.

"Not three seconds before that play happened," Stafford said, "I'm (talking) about, 'All right, let's answer back after this,' and he goes, 'Well, you don't know. (Murray) could throw one in there, it could be tipped and picked,' and as he's finishing the sentence, the damn thing happened."

After Jones' 31-yard return, the Rams went 68 yards to go in front for the first time on a 2-yard pass from Stafford to Odell Beckham Jr., giving the wide receiver touchdowns in three consecutive games.

The kickers were trading long field goals, Gay producing a season-best 55-yarder and later a 35-yarder.

The Rams' defense was doing better against Murray this time around. Donald recorded two of his sacks in the first half, giving him three in the past three quarters after he got to Jacksonville's Trevor Lawrence in the fourth quarter of the Rams' victory over the Jaguars. The makeshift secondary was holding the league's completion percentage leader below his norm.

Murray did pull out a signature play by running for 16 yards and stepping out of bounds at the Rams' 36 with one second left before halftime, allowing Matt Prater to kick a 53-yard field goal and make it 13-13.

The Rams got a scare at the end of the second half too when Prater kicked his third field goal with 37 seconds left, and the Cardinals recovered an on-side kick.

But Donald, who had started the game with a sack, ended it with his season-high third sack of the game with Arizona at its own 42-yard line.

"He stepped up," Floyd said, "like a lot of (Rams) players." ∎

DeAndre Hopkins (10) had only 54 yards receiving for the Cardinals, and his quarterback Kyler Murray was sacked four times to go along with two interceptions. (AP Images)

Rams 20, Seahawks 10
December 21, 2021 • Inglewood, California

SHORTEST PATH TO VICTORY

Kupp Continues Record-Setting Season with 9 Catches, 136 Yards

By Kevin Modesti

After the longest, strangest week of their season, the Rams took the shortest, straightest way to victory Tuesday night at SoFi Stadium.

They let Matthew Stafford and Cooper Kupp win a game for them.

The defense kept them in it. The ground game kept them moving. But when the Rams were tied with the Seattle Seahawks in the fourth quarter and desperate, they turned to what's been working all season.

"There's certain times in a game when you feel like you have to make a play," Stafford said. "I trusted Cooper to get there."

Kupp's 29-yard catch and run for a touchdown with Stafford's perfectly lofted pass on a first-down play with 11 minutes to go in the game broke a tie and sent the Rams to a 20-10 victory.

They'd waited two extra days to play the game, which was postponed because of the Rams' COVID-19 outbreak.

Waiting 3½ quarters to win seemed to only make the win more gratifying.

"It makes it that much sweeter when you see guys just stay connected, stay together," Rams coach Sean McVay said. "Guys didn't blink. They didn't flinch."

The Rams' third win in a row improved their record to 10-4, tied with the Arizona Cardinals atop the NFC West, although Arizona is still ahead on tiebreakers.

There were other heroes. The Rams' defense stopped the Seahawks (5-9) on downs at midfield with 3:21 to play. Matt Gay's second field goal of the night, his 20th successful kick in a row, added insurance. Sony Michel's fourth-down running capped his day of 92 yards on the ground and 23 in the air.

But in many ways, it was, yet again, Stafford's and Kupp's night.

A day after he was named to his first Pro Bowl, Kupp caught nine passes for 136 yards and two touchdowns, giving him 122 receptions this season to break Isaac Bruce's 26-year-old franchise record of 119.

Kupp became the first NFL receiver in the Super Bowl era to gain 90 yards or more in 10 consecutive games, breaking a record he had shared with Michael Irvin and now-teammate Odell Beckham Jr.

True to form, Kupp steered praise toward the pass in discussing the timing route that created the decisive touchdown.

"Matthew Stafford is a very good football player," Kupp said. "That's my analysis of that touchdown."

Stafford, who completed 21 of 29 passes for 244 yards, reached a milestone of his own, becoming the fastest quarterback to reach 50,000 career yards, doing it in his 182nd game.

Wide receiver Cooper Kupp paved the way for a Rams victory, catching nine passes for 136 yards and two touchdowns. (Los Angeles Daily News: Will Lester)

The Rams will end up with a bunch of Pro Bowlers this season by the time the rest of the selections are announced this week, but that didn't give them any privileges Tuesday.

As the old saying goes, on any given Tuesday any team hit hard by COVID-19 can beat any other team hit hard by COVID-19.

The Seahawks, seven-point underdogs, were looking confident when they went into halftime tied even as the Rams were out-gaining them 153 yards to 79, on the way to out-gaining them 332 to 214 for the game.

The Rams needed a running-into-the-punter penalty on their first drive to put them in position for Gay to kick a 55-yard field goal.

Then they squandered three trips inside the Seattle 40-yard line. From the 32, Stafford threw his first interception in three weeks on an underthrown deep ball to Kupp that was picked off by Quandre Diggs. From the 31, Stafford held the ball too long and was sacked to force a punt. Again from the 32, McVay decided to go for it on fourth-and-2, and a pass to Kupp was broken up.

After that decision by the Rams to pass up a field-goal attempt, the Seahawks went 59 yards and got a 39-yarder from Jason Myers with 10 seconds to go in the half.

But the Rams' defense was on the job. Sacks by Aaron Donald (giving him 10 in his eighth Pro Bowl season) and Von Miller (his first with the Rams) ended the Seahawks' first two possessions. Jalen Ramsey covered D.K. Metcalf and a third-down pass fell to the turf.

But the defense opened the second half by giving up a 75-yard, 11-play drive, DeeJay Dallas' 8-yard push through a gang of Rams tacklers putting Seattle at the 4 and Dallas' run over Leonard Floyd and Taylor Rapp putting it in the end zone.

Now they had an on-the-field challenge following the COVID-19 challenges of the past week.

At one point they had 29 players, including eight regular starters, on the NFL's COVID-19 reserve list.

Those numbers were down to 16 and three by Tuesday. Tight end Tyler Higbee, right tackle Rob Havenstein and safety Jordan Fuller were the starters who had failed to submit the negative tests required by a noon deadline to be activated.

With top offensive line backup Joe Noteboom also on the COVID list, Bobby Evans started in Havenstein's place. Center Brian Allen returned after missing most of two games with a knee injury. Stafford was sacked four times, but the line was solid in the running game.

Missing Fuller, their defensive signal-caller, the Rams turned to rookie Ernest Jones for that important duty and he did that and led the team with 11 tackles and a key late pass breakup.

As they had in beating the Cardinals last week with five players on the COVID list, the Rams leaned on backups and asked their leaders to take it up a notch.

Tuesday, when they needed it, that was Kupp and Stafford.

"It's a whole lot of trust," Stafford said of what made the decisive play work. "I had to cut it loose early, and cut it loose to a spot that I think only he's going to be able to get to.

"It turned out to be a good spot." ∎

Running back Sony Michel heads upfield for a large gain during the third quarter against the visiting Seahawks. (Los Angeles Daily News: Will Lester)

Rams 30, Vikings 23
December 26, 2021 • Minneapolis, Minnesota

AN UNLIKELY HERO

Punt Runback by Brandon Powell Highlights Playoff-Clinching Victory

By Kevin Modesti

The somersault that propelled the Rams to the playoffs was more than an expression of joy by an unlikely hero.

It was a fitting memory from a rough-and-tumble game in an increasingly head-over-heels season.

It happened when quarterback Matthew Stafford was struggling. When the offensive line and defense were bruised. When the Rams were straining to seize control against the Minnesota Vikings.

A punt return for a touchdown out of nowhere by Brandon Powell, a practice-squad call-up who has been with the team for only four games, gave the Rams control in the fourth quarter of what became a 30-23 victory at U.S. Bank Stadium in Minneapolis.

"We had to have that," Rams coach Sean McVay, rung out after a tense afternoon and hard couple of weeks, said of the game-defining play.

The victory clinched a playoff spot for the Rams (11-4) and gave them first place in the NFC West by one game over the Arizona Cardinals with two games to play.

It completed the Rams' turnaround from 0-3 in November to a 4-0 in December, accomplished despite missing starting players in each of the past three games because of COVID-19.

And it happened on a day when McVay's characteristic exuberance over a "great team win"

was never more justified, with all parts of the squad contributing, right down to Travin Howard, Alaric Jackson and Powell.

Powell's 61-yard run, untouched up the right sideline before he went head over heels over the goal line in celebration, was the Rams' first punt-return touchdown since one by Pharoh Cooper in 2017 and their biggest special-teams play of 2021.

It gave the Rams a 20-10 lead midway through the third quarter, before Stafford's 7-yard touchdown pass to Odell Beckham Jr. with 11:37 to play and Matt Gay's third field goal made them safe from two late scores by the Vikings.

Gay, who has been good on 23 field-goal tries in a row, was one of the Rams continuing to string together big games.

Cooper Kupp (10 receptions for 109 yards) set an NFL record with his 11th straight game of 90 yards or more. Sony Michel (131 yards and a touchdown on 27 carries) performed like a starter again, showing second and third effort on run after run. Aaron Donald (one sack, three tackles for loss) and Jalen Ramsey (holding Vikings receiver Justin Jefferson in check) performed like stars and leaders.

It was a gritty, bend-don't-break game by the defense, which held the Vikings to 2 for 11 on third-down

Brandon Powell flips into the end zone during a 61-yard punt return for a touchdown, sending the Rams into the postseason. (AP Images)

conversions and 3.0 yards per rush with Minnesota running back Dalvin Cook sidelined by COVID-19.

Playing much of the game without linebacker Ernest Jones (ankle) and lineman Greg Gaines (hand), against a Minnesota offense that was ninth in the NFL in yards and ranked seventh by Football Outsiders analytics, the Rams' defense set a resilient tone from the start.

Stops for short yardage by Jones and Donald made the Vikings punt quickly on the game's first drive, and the Rams took over and went 70 yards to go in front on Michel's twisting, stretching 1-yard touchdown.

After Jones went out, Howard took over at inside linebacker and made his first NFL interception, taking a tipped pass by Kirk Cousins in the end zone to turn Minnesota away on third and goal from the Rams' 8.

The Rams were up 10-0 on a field goal in the second quarter when Stafford, having escaped a rush, had a pass intercepted by Anthony Barr to set up the Vikings at the Rams' 11.

But Gaines sacked Cousins on first down, and the Rams held the Vikings to three points.

What the Rams got on offense, they were getting despite a makeshift line. Left tackle Andrew Whitworth and his backup Joe Noteboom both were on the COVID-19 reserve list, forcing David Edwards to move over from left guard and Coleman Shelton to come in at guard. Then center Brian Allen re-injured his right knee, putting Shelton at center and Edwards back at guard and bringing undrafted rookie Jackson in at left tackle for his first extended action.

"From how I was feeling in there, it felt like he stepped in and played great," Stafford said. "He's as even-keel as they come for a rookie. It helps (that) he's a giant human and can move and is strong."

The Vikings' pass rush didn't add to its league-leading 44 sacks but was a factor in two of Stafford's season-high three interceptions.

The third, the second by former UCLA linebacker Barr, was a pass tipped by Vikings defensive tackle Dalvin Tomlinson, who pushed Rams right guard Austin Corbett into the backfield.

A play later, Vikings running back Alexander Mattison had a 2-yard touchdown and the Rams' lead was cut to 13-10.

Stafford completed 21 of 37 passes for 197 yards and one touchdown while not being sacked, statistically his worst day with the Rams.

"Today was good team ball, but a lot to clean up in the pass game for us," Stafford said after qualifying for the playoffs, something he experienced three times in 12 seasons with the Detroit Lions. "I can definitely play way better."

Powell's play was his third touchdown but first on a return by the 26-year-old Florida product, a wide receiver and return man with the Lions (2018) and Atlanta Falcons (2020) before being released by the Buffalo Bills the Miami Dolphins this year and signed by the Rams in November.

The Rams had gone through seven punt and kicker returners before Powell announced his arrival with a 65-yard kickoff return on his first touch in L.A. against the Jacksonville Jaguars in Week 13.

"I just did the easy part," said Powell, clutching a game ball, crediting blocks by Grant Haley, Jake Funk and Michael Hoecht. "I just catch the ball and run."

Powell remembered the run but said he didn't remember somersaulting into the end zone.

"I just know I was happy as … I better watch my language," Powell said. "I was just happy to get in the end zone."

McVay was asked what he thought of the Powell's acrobatics.

"He can flip in as long as it's safe and there's nobody by him," McVay said.

With at least a wild card in their pocket, the Rams can't exactly cartwheel into the playoffs. They have to win out, on the road against the Baltimore Ravens and at SoFi Stadium against the San Francisco 49ers, to ensure themselves of the division title. It's the difference between being the NFC's No. 2 seed (right now), with home field in the first round, and No. 5, opening away.

"For our guys to be able to go undefeated in the month of December after the month of November we had, that says about as much about this group as you need to know," McVay said.

"We'll keep it rolling." ∎

Defensive tackle Aaron Donald pursues Vikings running back Alexander Mattison during the Rams' playoff-clinching victory. (AP Images)

Rams 20, Ravens 19

January 2, 2022 • Baltimore, Maryland

A THRILLER

Stafford Shakes Off 3 Turnovers, Throws Game-Winning Pass to Odell Beckham Jr.

By Kevin Modesti

This is not the way the Rams planned the party. It was almost spoiled when two Rams got into an altercation on the field in the game's first few minutes. It was almost ruined when Matthew Stafford and the offense were late showing up. It could have ended early when the Baltimore Ravens led by two scores in the fourth quarter at M&T Bank Stadium.

Stafford shook off three more turnovers, Cooper Kupp made it another record-setting day, and mid-season acquisitions Odell Beckham Jr. and Von Miller ended up heroes in a 20-19 victory.

But the day's cork-popping celebration was not to be.

In a game played later, the Arizona Cardinals beat the Dallas Cowboys to keep the Rams from clinching the NFC West with one week left on the regular-season schedule.

With their win, the Rams (12-4) did move closer to the division title and move up to No. 2 seed in the NFC. Now the Rams will need a win over the San Francisco 49ers or a loss by Arizona (11-5) at home to the Seattle Seahawks to take first place. Otherwise, they Rams will lose the division on tiebreakers and be wild cards, forced to open the playoffs on the road.

Given what they've overcome during their late-season winning streak, including the COVID-19 outbreak that kept numerous starters out of the win over the Cardinals, it was almost fitting that this win was more of an ordeal than a party.

"It's a really, really resilient group, and guys made plays when we had to," said safety Jordan Fuller, whose interception late in the first half was one of the biggest.

Miller's play was a sack of Tyler Huntley on first down from the Baltimore 38 with 19 seconds on the clock that basically ended the Ravens' hope for their own winning drive.

Beckham's two plays were a brilliant catch for a first down followed by a catch, run and stretch to the right end-zone pylon to give the Rams the lead with 57 seconds to play.

Until then, the Ravens (8-8) had been in front for 46 minutes, going up 0-0 in the second quarter and 16-7 heading to the fourth after a Stafford fumble led to the third of Justin Tucker's four field goals.

But Stafford was already sixth in the NFL since 1960 with 33 fourth-quarter comebacks and eighth with 41 game-winning drives, and he went to work on a 34th by looking for Kupp.

Kupp's 21-yard catch and run to the Ravens' 8 set up a short run by Sony Michel for a touchdown that made it a two-point game with 12:09 to play.

It also gave Kupp the Rams record for receiving yards in a season, his 1,829 by the end of the day surpassing Isaac Bruce's 1,781 in 1995.

Odell Beckham Jr. stretches toward the end zone for a touchdown, giving the Rams the lead with 57 seconds remaining. (AP Images)

The Ravens marched right back up the field before Aaron Donald and Leonard Floyd teamed up on one of the Rams' five sacks to hold Baltimore to three points and keep it a five-point game with 4:30 to play.

Stafford came through, and this time it was Beckham instead of Kupp making the big play. Beckham's great, two-handed catch over his head for a first down made it first down at the 7. The touchdown was almost anti-climatic after that catch.

"I got it tatted on the off-season," Beckham said afterward. "It says, 'Pressure: I Live for It.' It's just those moments when you're so locked in to the game and you know you have an opportunity.

"I don't really think that I'm thinking, 'Division is on the line. The game (is on the line).' You're thinking about just the game at the moment. 'We've got to make this play.'"

It set up as a day for the Rams to take their biggest step yet toward what they hope will be an appearance in the Super Bowl LVI on home turf at SoFi Stadium on Feb. 13.

Having clinched at least a playoff wild card last week, they hoped to wrap up their third division title in coach Sean McVay's five seasons. If the Rams won, McVay had said, they might delay takeoff for their charter flight home so they could watch the Cardinals game if it was going the right way. (It wasn't, and the plane took off before the Cardinals completed their 25-22 win.)

McVay had also cautioned against the Rams getting ahead of themselves. And they spent the first half showing why by falling behind against an opponent that had lost four in a row and was playing with quarterback Lamar Jackson sidelined by an ankle injury.

The game was only five plays old when TV replays showed Rams cornerback Jalen Ramsey shoving safety Taylor Rapp after a 13-yard pass play. Later replays showed coaches and teammates separately trying to calm Ramsey and Rapp on the sideline. It was a jarring image of a defense that had been coming together late in the season.

McVay tried to downplay the incident.

"It's two great competitors. They both want to do right. There's a little bit of a mix-up right there," McVay said.

"Ever get into a fight with your brother? Yeah, you did.

"They moved on, and they kept it going."

On offense, it was one of those days when Stafford and his receivers weren't quite sharp at the start. Two incompletions forced the Rams into a 56-yard field-goal attempt by Matt Gay that missed to the right. That ended Gay's streak of 23 successful field-goal attempts.

Then it got worse.

Stafford threw another of the disastrous interceptions that have plagued his otherwise strong first season with the Rams. Trying to hit Tyler Higbee over the middle on third and 2 at the Rams' 16, Stafford threw it to Ravens safety Chuck Clark, who ran it back for the first score of the game. It was Stafford's fourth pick-six of the year.

Next possession, Stafford under-threw a deep pass to Odell Beckham Jr. and had it picked off by Clark at the Ravens' 4. It was Stafford's fifth interception in his last five quarters.

"I hate going over all these, to be honest with you. I'm tired of doing it," Stafford said with grim good humor as he recounted his interceptions and later fumble on a day he finished with 26 completions in 35 attempts for 309 yards and two touchdowns.

The Ravens drove 91 yards before a pass rush by Donald forced Huntley into a high throw into the end zone, and Baltimore settled for a field goal and a 10-0 lead.

The Rams might have felt some momentum after Fuller intercepted a Huntley pass to give Stafford the ball at the Ravens' 29, and an 18-yard catch and run by Kupp made it 10-7.

But the Ravens took the kickoff with 52 seconds to play in the first half, and Huntley drove them 51 yards to a 46-yard field goal and a 13-7 lead at halftime.

The Rams' chances would get worse — before they got better.

"Wow, what a great, gutsy win," McVay said. "It certainly wasn't perfect, but you talk about playing as a team, picking each other up as a team when you needed it.

"We found a lot of different ways to do things that we can't do as we move forward (in the playoffs), but we ended up overcoming it."

They'll drink to that. Just not champagne yet. ∎

Matthew Stafford reacts as running back Sony Michel rushes for a touchdown during the second half in Baltimore. (AP Images)

10

WIDE RECEIVER

COOPER KUPP

Rams' Cooper Kupp Gained Healthy Perspective from Waiting

February 10, 2022 | By Kevin Modesti

The best way for a great football player to enhance his reputation is to rise to the occasion in the Super Bowl.

Three years ago, Cooper Kupp picked the worst way. He enhanced his reputation by missing the Super Bowl.

He didn't really pick that path, of course. Kupp missed the Rams' last nine games of the 2018 regular season and postseason after tearing his left ACL. When the Rams lost that Super Bowl to the Patriots 13-3, it wasn't the first sign but it was the most painful reminder of what the wide receiver meant to their offense.

Three years later, as Kupp gets his first chance to play in a Super Bowl on Sunday at SoFi Stadium against the Cincinnati Bengals, he's still thinking about the one he had to watch from the Rams' sideline in Atlanta.

"Missing that Super Bowl, that's one of the hardest things I've been through," Kupp said a few days ago. "The conflict it creates in you, when you're both cheering and pulling for your guys, but you know that every time they do succeed it just hurts you that much more because you want to be a part of it as well."

In 2018, Kupp was in his second season with the Rams after being drafted in the third round out of Eastern Washington, and the son and grandson of NFL players was just starting to prove himself in the pros.

He's on a different level now. At 28, he's going into the final game of a breakout year, one of the best ever by a receiver. Setting records was practically a weekly occurrence in the second half of the regular season.

Kupp rocketed to the top of the Rams' all-time receiving lists in the NFL's first 17-game season: His 145 receptions are an indisputable Rams record, surpassing Isaac Bruce and Tory Holt. His 1,947 yards are a Rams record, although not as good on a per-game basis as Elroy Hirsch's 1,495 in 12 games in 1951 and Jim Benton's 1,067 in nine games in 1945. His 16 touchdowns are second to Hirsch's 17 in '51.

Perhaps not coincidentally, Bruce and Holt were stars of the Rams' only Super Bowl-winning team, when they were the St. Louis Rams in 1999, Hirsch was a star of the Los Angeles Rams' only NFL championship-winning team in 1951, and Benton was a star of the franchise's first NFL championship as the Cleveland Rams in 1945.

Cooper Kupp waves to the SoFi Stadium crowd following a loss to the San Francisco 49ers in Week 16. The Rams would go on to claim the NFC Championship against the 49ers as well as the Super Bowl on home turf. (Los Angeles Daily News: David Crane)

Kupp also became the first player since the Panthers' Steve Smith in 2005, and the 12th in NFL and AFL history, to lead a league's receivers in catches, yards and touchdowns.

He can become the first receiving Triple Crown winner to earn a Super Bowl ring in the same season, and join Hirsch in 1951, the Packers' Don Hutson in 1944 and the Colts' Raymond Berry in 1959 as the only Triple Crown winners to capture a pre-Super Bowl-era NFL championship in the same season.

Part of what makes Kupp unique is that he consistently, seemingly genuinely puts a lower priority than most people do on enhancing his reputation or achieving personal glory.

As hard as it was to miss Super Bowl LIII, he says the experience taught him an enduring lesson. It's a version of: Since the destination is uncertain, you'd better enjoy the journey.

"Not being able to play in that first Super Bowl back in 2019 offered a pretty cool perspective for me (on) the importance of enjoying the process of what this NFL season is," Kupp said.

"I've really been able to take the approach this year that every single day I get to come in here (to the Rams' training facility), being able to play alongside the guys I get to play with, the coaches that come in here, (that's) the important thing."

Kupp said he didn't take lightly the chance to play for a championship, especially after missing the chance before.

"(But) the important things from that year to me was the people I got to spend that time around, and the enjoyment of the process, and coming in and spending 12, 13, 14 hours or whatever it is preparing alongside these guys to play a football game," he said. "That's the stuff that I really enjoyed."

Coaches and teammates marvel at Kupp's enthusiasm for learning about the game that was handed down to him by his father, Craig, a quarterback who got into one game for the Cardinals in 1991, and grandfather, Jake, a Pro Bowl guard who played for the Saints and three other teams in the 1960s and '70s.

Cooper Kupp celebrates a first-down catch against the Arizona Cardinals during the regular season. (Los Angeles Daily News: Terry Pierson)

Kupp watches game film with Matthew Stafford so he can see it through his quarterback's eyes. He watches offensive linemen for tips on blocking, which is part of his game. He turned his knee injury to his advantage by taking his recovery time to improve pass-running techniques.

"I think the thing that probably got him there is all the work that he puts into it, and I'm glad it's paying off for him," Stafford said.

Kupp says his dedication comes from what he calls a "supernatural calling" to football.

"I think that really comes down to my faith," Kupp said. "I believe God made me with a purpose. He gave me the passions and the talents to pursue a specific thing. I feel like I found that at a young age. I just felt like when I was playing football, he was well pleased with what I was doing.

"It was really about, each day, waking up and saying I want to be the best that I can possibly be for no other reason than that God has put me here and I want to honor that and respect that to the best of my abilities. So I get to come in to work with the greatest purpose, the greatest drive and the greatest goals in mind."

As for why Kupp made the leap to his first Pro Bowl and All-Pro selections this season, part of the credit goes to the addition of Stafford in the offseason.

Part goes to Kupp staying healthy enough to play every game for first time in his five NFL seasons. The 6-foot-2, 208-pound receiver showed up at training camp looking more muscular than before. (Such was the effect that reporters watching from the sidelines thought he looked taller, too.)

Now there's one more game.

Kupp, born in 1993 – the last year the Super Bowl was played in the Los Angeles area, the Cowboys beating the Bills 52-17 at the Rose Bowl – grew up with the Super Bowl "basically another holiday" in his family.

He dreamed, vaguely, of playing in the Super Bowl someday.

"None of those dreams were filled with any anxiety. Those dreams were always filled with the joy of the moment," Kupp said. "I'm going to enjoy every second of playing in this game." ∎

Cooper Kupp gains control of the ball while pursued by 49ers players Jimmie Ward and Emmanuel Moseley. (Los Angeles Daily News: David Crane)

Rams 34, Cardinals 11
January 17, 2022 • Inglewood, California

WILDEST DREAMS

Rams, Matthew Stafford Take Care of Ball and Cardinals

By Kevin Modesti

Going into the Rams' first-round matchup against the Arizona Cardinals, the question was whether Matthew Stafford could finally win a playoff game.

Coming out of it, the question is why he would stop with just one.

Playoff Stafford turns out to be the best Stafford all season.

Passing for two touchdowns, sneaking for another and letting the Rams' defense pressure Cardinals quarterback Kyler Murray into the big mistakes, Stafford led a 34-11 victory in an NFC wild-card game in front of a noisy crowd of 70,625 at SoFi Stadium.

"It felt like the ball was going to the right place, and our guys made great plays," Stafford said. "That's how I expect to go out and play every game. It doesn't always work out that way."

The fourth-seeded Rams (13-5) advance to face the second-seeded Buccaneers at Tampa Bay (14-4).

The fifth-seeded Cardinals (11-7) and Murray take their regrets home to Phoenix after losing for the fifth time in six games.

It wasn't as if the Rams were thrilled with how they finished the regular season, either, blowing a 17-point first-half lead and losing to the San Francisco 49ers in their finale.

But after lectures from their coaches during the week about starting and finishing strong, and avoiding the turnovers that can let a team back in a game, the Rams showed what happens when they do all that.

The Rams led 21-0 before the Cardinals recorded a first down.

The Rams led 28-0 after Stafford hit Cooper Kupp for a 7-yard touchdown to cap their first drive of the second half.

The Rams' riskiest pass of the night was thrown not by Stafford but by wide receiver Odell Beckham Jr., who took Stafford's lateral pass and threw deep to Cam Akers for a 40-yard gain to set up the Kupp touchdown.

Akers was on his way to a night that capped his quick comeback from an Achilles' tendon injury in July. Akers had got his feet wet with a few carries and catches against the 49ers. On Monday he stretched his legs, rushing 17 times for 55 yards and catching the one pass for 40, while Sony Michel ran 13 times for 58.

And Stafford was on his way to the cleanest and best playoff performance of his career, completing 13 of 17 passes for 202 yards, two touchdowns and no

Matthew Stafford runs for yardage during the fourth quarter of the Rams' rout of the Cardinals.
(Los Angeles Daily News: David Crane)

interceptions while being sacked only once.

The 17 passes were Stafford's fewest this season, but his 154.5 passer rating was his highest since his 156.1 in the Rams' season-opening victory over the Bears.

It was his first outing without an interception in five games, after he tied for the NFL lead in interceptions during the regular season.

Stafford's performance was the product of a game plan and the running game keeping the Rams out of third-and-long trouble, and the quarterback's own effort.

"Matthew made great decisions. I think it's good so you don't have to talk about that anymore," McVay joked to reporters about the frequent questions about Stafford's lack of playoff wins. "Really proud of him.

"I thought he did a great job, number one. But we were able to stay in those kind of manageable situations. I thought it was a really good, complementary football game that we played."

Both quarterbacks were seeking their first playoff victories, Stafford having gone 0-3 in 12 years in Detroit and Murray having reached the postseason for the first time in three years in Arizona.

One looked the part, wide-eyed in the Monday night spotlight. Murray threw two interceptions in the first half. The first was a disastrous mistake.

Trailing 14-0, still looking for Arizona's initial first down after four possessions, Murray faded back into his own end zone on a third-and-7 and was set upon by inside linebacker Troy Reeder. Desperate to avoid being tackled for a safety, Murray flung the ball to the right end of the Cardinals' line. No Cardinal was close to catching it.

Rams cornerback David Long charged in, grabbed it at ankle level and trotted in for a 3-yard touchdown.

It would take a sixth Cardinals possession for them to get into positive yardage. The Rams' defense set the tone by sacking Murray twice in the first half. Von Miller recorded his sixth sack in the Rams' past five games, and Aaron Donald

Odell Beckham Jr. pulls in a touchdown catch during the Rams' explosive first quarter of the NFC wild-card game. (Los Angeles Daily News: David Crane)

and Greg Gaines shared one. The secondary was solid, despite having to bring Eric Weddle out of retirement with starting safeties Jordan Fuller and Taylor Rapp both sidelined.

On offense, all Stafford had to do was avoid giveaways, and he did.

After the defense gave him the ball near midfield, Stafford's perfectly lofted pass hit Beckham in the left corner of the end zone for a 4-yard touchdown and a 7-0 lead.

"I trusted myself, trusted my abilities, trusted my teammates to just go out there and play," Stafford said, "and let the chips fall where they may."

Everything, for Stafford and all the Rams, might get harder when they go on the road to face Tom Brady and the Super Bowl champions.

But if Stafford plays with the same self-control, the Rams have a chance.

"I thought he did a great job leading the way," McVay said. ∎

Above: Rams head coach Sean McVay waits for the result of a disputed call during the second quarter. Opposite: Sony Michel thought he'd scored during the first quarter, but the play was called back. The Rams nonetheless jumped to a 21-0 lead before the Cardinals could record a first down. (Los Angeles Daily News: David Crane)

3

WIDE RECEIVER

ODELL BECKHAM JR.

Beckham Advances in the Playoffs for the First Time While Earning Teammates' Respect

January 21, 2022 | By Kevin Modesti

Odell Beckham Jr. has been full of surprises since joining the Rams, on and off the field. But maybe they shouldn't be surprises.

When the wide receiver took a lateral pass from Matthew Stafford, turned and threw a pass of his own to Cam Akers for a 40-yard gain to set up a touchdown early in the second half against the Arizona Cardinals, the play had many looking up Beckham's history of throwing the ball.

It turns out he completed four of six passes for 144 yards and two touchdowns with the New York Giants and Cleveland Browns, connecting for a 57-yard score to Saquon Barkley in 2018 for New York.

"I think I gave Saquon a better pass than I gave Cam. So (I'm) just happy that we connected on it," Beckham said Friday as the Rams prepared to go on the road to face the Tampa Bay Buccaneers in the second round of the playoffs.

Beckham said the Rams practiced the play, but it was a windy day at Cal Lutheran University and his pass missed Akers. So he wasn't sure Coach Sean McVay would call it in a game.

"Sometimes those types of things happen and it's taken out (of the game plan)," Beckham said. "He was like, 'I'm calling it.' And I was like, 'Bet. I'm (going to) be ready to go.'"

Even real quarterbacks were impressed.

"Odell is a super talented guy," Rams quarterback Matthew Stafford said. "He made that throw right-handed. He could probably do it lefty, too. He's a freak.

"Kudos to Sean for calling it that time. It was an awesome call."

Said Rams offensive coordinator Kevin O'Connell, a former NFL backup: "When he throws that tight of a spiral and that nose just turns over like that, the first thing you deep down think is jealousy. 'Why couldn't I have thrown the ball like that?'"

In his day job, as a wide receiver, Beckham has helped the Rams survive the season-ending injury to Robert Woods with five touchdown receptions in eight games since he signed with his third NFL team after agreeing to be released by the Browns in mid-November.

As striking has been the way he has impressed other Rams in the locker room and meeting rooms by living

Odell Beckham Jr. was a huge midseason addition to the Rams and a big part of making up for the loss of Robert Woods to a season-ending injury. (AP Images)

down a reputation for being what Beckham himself called "a 'me' guy."

Stafford called him a "great teammate" and McVay called him a "joy to be around" last week, and McVay on Friday held the door open to re-signing Beckham, whose contract expires after the season.

Cornerback Jalen Ramsey said Thursday that Beckham is "like the offensive version of myself," beyond their talents.

"He's kind of misunderstood too," Ramsey said. "He's a really good teammate, and people kind of don't have that message out about him, but he really is a really good teammate.

"He's just super competitive, and wants to be great, and wants everybody around him to be great."

Asked about that, Beckham said he has accepted that some people see him as selfish.

"It's not from like y'all (media) that I feel misunderstood," Beckham said. "I'm always just going to be that. Since I came into the league, there's been drama – this, that. Like, bro, it's (just) something that I've gotten over.

"I know who I am. I feel like once you get comfortable with being in your own skin, and you know who you are on the outside, and things that could be said and this and that, it means absolutely nothing. And to me, it means absolutely nothing."

The Rams' 34-11 victory over Arizona in the wild-card round, in which Beckham caught four passes for 54 yards and the opening touchdown, was his first NFL playoff victory. Having joined the L.A. offense about a month after the Rams beat the Bucs, 34-24, in September, he could play a big role in the postseason. Though another trick play seems unlikely.

As for why perceptions of him might be changing since he came to the Rams, Beckham said: "I think winning cures everything." ■

Odell Beckham Jr. hauls in a touchdown in the NFL wild-card win over Arizona, the first playoff win of Beckham's career. [AP Images]

Rams 30, Buccaneers 27
January 23, 2022 • Tampa, Florida

BYE BYE BRADY

Rams Pull Out of Tailspin to Beat Tampa Bay

By Kevin Modesti

Another magical pass and catch by Matthew Stafford and Cooper Kupp put the Rams a kick away from victory, and coach Sean McVay's reaction on the sideline was unprintable.

"If I said (what it was), I'd get fined," McVay said with a grin.

Stafford rushed to the line of scrimmage and spiked the ball to stop the clock with four seconds remaining, and his exact reaction as he ran off the field is lost in the emotion of the moment.

"I don't know what I said, to be honest with you," Stafford said, laughing as if he just didn't want to say. "I was enjoying the moment."

The latest clutch field goal by Matt Gay sealed the Rams' heart-stopping win, and defensive star Aaron Donald's thoughts as he watched defied his usual clear-headed stoicism.

"You're happy," Donald said, "but it's like, 'Oh, my god.'"

The Rams' 30-27, divisional-round playoff victory over the Tampa Bay Buccaneers at unusually chilly, windy Raymond James Stadium on Sunday could not be summed up in any single word, or four letters, or any length.

It was soaring, the Rams building a 27-3 lead with seven minutes to play in the third quarter and looking as if they'd not just knock off but humiliate seven-time Super Bowl winner Tom Brady and the defending-champion Buccaneers.

It was frightening, four Rams fumbles and a missed field goal letting Brady and the Bucs roar back to tie the game on a fourth-down touchdown run by Leonard Fournette with 42 seconds to play.

It was almost unbelievable, the way Stafford caught the Bucs in a poorly executed blitz and found Kupp deep for a 44-yard gain that put the Rams at the 12, with no timeouts but just enough time to execute the spike and set up the kick.

No matter how they did it, by any name or description, it was a rose of a victory that sent the Rams on to the NFC championship game against the San Francisco 49ers at SoFi Stadium.

"There are no style points in the playoffs," McVay said.

The Rams overcame Brady and the Bucs in their stadium, ending Tampa Bay's reign and stamping their own Super Bowl credentials.

And they overcame their own disasters.

Leading the way on offense was Stafford, who won his first playoff game in 13 NFL seasons when the Rams beat the Cardinals last Monday but was really at his best Sunday. Stafford completed 28 of 38 passes for 366 yards,

Aaron Donald sacks Tampa Bay quarterback Tom Brady during the first half their NFC divisional-round playoff game. (AP Images)

two touchdowns and no interceptions.

The first big play was a 70-yard pass-and-run to Kupp that put the Rams ahead 17-3 early in the second quarter. Kupp finished with nine catches for 183 yards, a season high in one of the great seasons for an NFL wide receiver.

Leading on defense was Donald, who had one of the Rams' three sacks of Brady as the pass rush did what it had to do by putting constant pressure on the quarterback.

Ahead 20-3 at halftime, the Rams got the first score of the third quarter on Stafford's 1-yard sneak to make it look like a runaway at 27-3.

The Bucs chipped away with Ryan Succop's second field goal, and then took advantage of Kupp's first fumble of the 2021 season to march 30 yards to a 1-yard Fournette touchdown run, cutting the Rams' lead to 27-13 going to the fourth quarter.

L.A. nerves started to tighten, and the crowd of 65,597 came to life.

"I knew it was going to come down to the end," said Rams linebacker Von Miller, who had a sack. "All the times I've played Tom Brady, I knew no lead that we had was safe."

Gay's miss of a 47-yard field-goal attempt that would have made it a three-score lead with 6:31 to play kept the Bucs alive.

Brady hit Mike Evans, beating cornerback Jalen Ramsey, for a 55-yard touchdown pass to cut the Rams' lead to 27-20 with 3:20 to play.

A fumble by running back Cam Akers then gave the Bucs the ball at the Rams' 30 with 2:25 to play.

That was too much of an opening to give Brady, who guided Tampa Bay to the tying touchdown.

Both teams went into the divisional-round game with star offensive linemen injured, the Rams missing left tackle Andrew Whitworth and the Bucs right tackle Tristan Wirfs.

From the start, the Rams handled it and the Bucs couldn't.

Stafford found seven different receivers in the first half, including third-year tight end Kendall Blanton, whose 7-yard touchdown to make it 10-0 in the first quarter was his first in the NFL.

Rams outside linebacker Von Miller strips the ball from Tom Brady as the Rams withstood the Bucs' comeback bid. (AP Images)

The Bucs were the defending champions, and Brady is the seven-time Super Bowl winner, but you couldn't tell from their lack of poise in the first half.

Tampa Bay drew three after-the-play penalties, each for 15 yards. The third was on Brady for screaming at an official after he didn't get a call after a heavy pass rush. TV showed Brady with a bloodied lower lip.

It was a fitting image on a day Brady finished with 30 completions in 54 attempts for 329 yards, one touchdown and one interception.

"You know, in the end, they just made one more play than us," Brady said.

The last big play, the 44-yard pass to Kupp, came on what NFL people call a "love of the game route." Meaning a receiver has to love the game to want to run it. It's almost always a decoy, meant to help someone else get open.

This time, Kupp caught the Bucs without deep coverage on first down from the Rams' 44, one play after he caught a 20-yarder and got out of bounds with 28 seconds left.

"Some guys didn't blitz," Tampa Bay coach Bruce Arians said. "I don't know if we didn't get the call (from the sideline to the players), but was an all-out blitz (and) should have had a lot of pressure."

"It seemed like (the ball) hung up there forever," Kupp said, echoing something McVay said.

Gay's field goal from 30 yards was his third of the game, to go with the one miss. The Rams poured onto the field as the clock struck :00.

Their Super Bowl path doesn't get easier. The Rams (14-5, including two playoff wins) have lost to the 49ers (12-7) the last six times the teams have met.

"But let's not talk about that right now," Miller said, looking forward to a celebratory flight home.

"I'm still trying to process everything." ∎

Matt Gay kicks the game-winning field goal after the Rams survived the Buccaneers' late-game efforts. (AP Images)

99
DEFENSIVE TACKLE

AARON DONALD
Donald Becomes the Rams' Super Motivator

January 28, 2022 | By Kevin Modesti

Aaron Donald has always led by example, quietly showing the rest of the Rams how to train, practice and play, even if few will ever do any of it at his level.

But teammates are seeing something different from the All-Pro defensive tackle in the week leading up to the Rams' NFC championship game against the San Francisco 49ers at SoFi Stadium.

Better yet, they're hearing something different.

Aaron Donald is leading by talking.

"And when he talks, everyone listens," Rams defensive coordinator Raheem Morris said. "The old E.F. Hutton deal."

Morris and the Rams' players say Donald is stepping up to deliver end-of-practice motivational messages. Huddling with individuals to whom he usually isn't close. Spreading his sense of urgency to the rest of the squad.

Donald says one reason for the change is that Von Miller, the outside linebacker acquired in November to complete form a pass-rushing dynamic duo, urged him to take advantage of his stature in football by speaking up more.

"One thing Von challenged me a lot more with is being more vocal. Talking to guys, letting them hear my voice," Donald said.

No explanation was needed for the other reason Donald finds it harder to stay quiet now.

The NFC title game puts Donald one win from returning to the Super Bowl and taking a second crack at winning the championship that eluded him when the Rams lost to the New England Patriots, 13-3, after the 2018 season.

At age 30, with three NFL Defensive Player of the Year awards, a Rams-record seven first-team All-Pro honors and the post-1982 Rams-record 98 regular-season sacks to his name, Donald doesn't have much else to accomplish.

"I know what it's like to be in it (the Super Bowl). I don't know what it's like to win," Donald said. "The only thing I'm lacking now is being a world champion.

"But to get to that point, we've got to win this week."

Aaron Donald celebrates a stop against San Francisco 49ers quarterback Jimmy Garoppolo during the NFC Championship Game. (Los Angeles Daily News: Keith Birmingham)

Eleven other current Rams were on the 2018 team that fell just short. As Donald points out, left tackle Andrew Whitworth, who was on that team, and quarterback Matthew Stafford, who joined the Rams in 2021, have been in the NFL longer than him and haven't won a Super Bowl. The same goes for longtime L.A. punter Johnny Hekker and safety Eric Weddle.

Yet it's Donald, specifically, whose Super Bowl quest seems to have become motivation for the whole team.

Miller, who was the MVP of the Denver Broncos' Super Bowl victory over the Carolina Panthers after the 2015 season, said he wants to help Donald have that experience.

"I want to complete the checklist for him," Miller said Wednesday. "Selfishly, that's what I want. I want to be the guy to say, 'Man, I helped A.D. get a Super Bowl.

"We want it for him. The whole team wants it for him. We're going to do everything we possibly can to get it done."

Morris, hired in 2021, remembered watching as the Rams lost to the Green Bay Packers in a divisional-round playoff game last season.

"I remember watching Aaron Donald's face, because they kept showing him on television, and I just looked into his eyes and felt that hurt and felt that pain," Morris said. "First thing I told him when I got here was, 'I'm going to do everything possible to help you win a championship.'"

Morris said there's a reason teammates rally around Donald.

"He's a humble guy. He's a great teammate to his guys. He does everything the right way, the way he trains," Morris said. "We love him. Just, flat-ass, we love him."

Donald says he appreciates hearing that.

Always one to lead by example, Aaron Donald stepped up as a more vocal leader during the Rams' championship season, thanks to encouragement from teammates like Von Miller. (Los Angeles Daily News: Keith Birmingham)

The 49ers haven't been as kind. They've done a good job of frustrating Donald lately, holding him to one sack of quarterback Jimmy Garoppolo in four meetings in 2020 and 2021 while extending their winning streak against the Rams to six games. The most recent Rams loss in the series might have been the most crushing, San Francisco wiping out a 17-0 deficit to win, 27-24, in overtime at SoFi Stadium on Jan. 9.

Donald is determined it won't happen again.

"My mindset is there's no way we're going to lose this game," he told reporters. "We've got to play for four quarters, and we've got to find a way to finish, and I know we're going to do that."

In a sign of his teammates' respect, Morris recalled seeing Ramsey sprint to join a pre-practice huddle when he saw Donald was talking to the group.

Ramsey said Donald was talking about keeping the team's focus on its Super Bowl goal and doing everything possible to achieve it.

Said Ramsey: "It does mean a little bit extra when A.D. does things like that." ∎

With three NFL Defensive Player of the Year awards and a franchise-record seven first-team All-Pro honors, a Super Bowl victory represented one of the last remaining achievements for the Rams' star defensive tackle. (Los Angeles Daily News: Keith Birmingham)

Rams 20, 49ers 17

January 30, 2022 • Inglewood, California

'LONG TIME COMING'

Rams Rally to Beat 49ers and Reach the Super Bowl on Home Turf

By Kevin Modesti

The Rams are going to — that is, staying for — the Super Bowl.

Doing it in a fashion both familiar and fresh, they rallied from a 10-point deficit in the fourth quarter to beat the San Francisco 49ers 20-17 in the NFC championship game in front of 73,202 Rams and Niners fans at SoFi Stadium.

Now it will be the Rams vs. the Cincinnati Bengals in Super Bowl LVI on the same field Feb. 13, with the "home" team opening as 3-1/2-point favorites.

"Love this team. We've got one more," said Rams coach Sean McVay, ebullient outside a raucous post-game locker room, as he began to look ahead to his second Super Bowl in four years and a chance to win his first.

The familiar part was quarterback Matthew Stafford and wide receiver Cooper Kupp combining for a 25-yard pass and run to set up an attempt at a tie-breaking field goal, and Matt Gay coming through with the 30-yard kick with 1:46 on the clock.

The same heroes and similar heroics, right down to the distance of the field goal, had beaten Tom Brady and the Buccaneers in the divisional playoff round the week before to put the Rams in the conference title game against their NFC West rivals.

Stafford completed 31 of 45 passes for 337 yards, two touchdowns and an interception Sunday. Kupp had

11 catches for 142 yards and two scores. Wide receiver Odell Beckham Jr. had his best game as a Ram, catching nine passes for 113 yards.

Stafford was emotional as the team celebrated on the field.

"Long time coming," said Stafford, who had never even won a playoff game before the trade that sent him from the Lions to the Rams a year ago Sunday. "It's been a lot of years in this league, and I've loved every minute of it.

"I'm happy for this (Super Bowl) opportunity, for not only myself but really so many guys in this locker room who deserve it."

The fact the Rams will play the Super Bowl at SoFi Stadium, trying to follow last season's Bucs and be the second team to win the title on home turf, was only a bonus to Stafford.

"I mean, it's great that it's here," Stafford said. "I don't give a s— where it is. I'm like, I just want to play in the dang thing. But the fact that it's under this roof, it's going to be awesome."

The fresh features of this victory included the Rams doing this against the 49ers, who had won the past six meetings between the team in the regular season.

And there were contributions from some less-well-known members of the Rams' star-studded roster. Tight

Odell Beckham Jr. had his best game as a Ram, catching nine passes for 113 yards. (Los Angeles Daily News: Keith Birmingham)

end Kendall Blanton had a career-high five catches for 57 yards, one to convert a third down on the game-winning drive. Linebacker Trevin Howard intercepted a tipped pass by Jimmy Garoppolo in the final minute to seal the win.

And a public show of the new, vocal leadership style of defensive tackle Aaron Donald, whose yearning for a Super Bowl title to top off his accomplishments has inspired him to make himself heard more during these playoffs.

With the Rams trailing 17-7, Donald gathered defensive teammates around him on the sideline and delivered what looked like a passionate speech. TV didn't pick up what he was saying. But he had everyone's attention.

"I don't remember (his) exact words," cornerback Jalen Ramsey said, "but, you know, kind of just like: How bad do we want it? We're right here. We got to do more. We got to give a little bit extra. We got to give more.

"And we just kind of went out there and did that, really."

The Rams' defense kept the 49ers off the scoreboard for the game's last 17 minutes, a turnaround on the Niners' big comeback to an overtime victory in the teams' last regular-season meeting.

"Today was a great sign of resilience," McVay said. "We've talked about (how) that's one of the things that's kind of embodied this group. We go down 17-7, it doesn't look good. But the guys just stayed in the moment. One play at a time, they did a great job.

"And then for the defense to be able to close it out, especially after the last time we played them, the way that went."

The 49ers took their 10-point lead when Garoppolo hit tight end George Kittle for a 15-yard touchdown with 1:59 to play in the third.

The 49ers had gotten the ball after a ruling that could have been pivotal.

Stafford tried to sneak for a first down on fourth and 1 at the Niners' 43 and was marked short of the line to gain. McVay threw the challenge flag. The review confirmed the ruling.

But after the Kittle touchdown, the Rams cut the 49ers' lead to 17-14 when Stafford connected with Kupp for 11 yards and their second score of the day with 13:30 to go in the game.

The Rams' defense forced a punt, and the offense drove from its own 15 to tie the game 7-17 with 6:49 to play on a 40-yard field goal by Gay.

Aaron Donald celebrates the Rams punching their ticket to Super Bowl LVI. (Los Angeles Daily News: Keith Birmingham)

The drive was helped along by an unnecessary-roughness penalty on Ward for a late hit on Beckham.

It was a physical game befitting the stakes and the old rivalry. Rams safety Nick Scott laid out 49ers wide receiver Deebo Samuel with a clean hit over the middle. Samuel was held under 100 yards receiving and rushing, but there was no preventing him from having an impact.

The 49ers led at halftime 10-7 after a defensive display that allowed for just enough of the pass-receiving stars that the decidedly mixed crowd of Rams and 49ers fans came paid big bucks to see.

Stafford forced a pass to Kupp at the goal line on third down at the 49ers' three in the first quarter, but cornerback K'Waun Williams got a hand on it and Ward intercepted it.

After a 49ers punt pinned the Rams back at their 3, running back Cam Akers and Sony Michel got the ball close to midfield, and then Stafford went back to Kupp. Completions for seven and 15 yards put the ball at the 13. A sack of Stafford made it third and 13.

Stafford lofted a pass to the right corner of the end zone, where Kupp made a tumbling catch behind cornerback Emanuel Moseley to put the Rams ahead 7-0 with 8:46 to play in the half, capping an 18-play, 97-yard drive.

There aren't too many answers to Kupp, but the 49ers have one in Samuel.

On the Niners' next drive, on second down and 7 at the L.A. 44, Garoppolo threw to Samuel behind the line of scrimmage, and he weaved through the secondary to tie the game 7-7 with 6:10 to go in the half.

The touchdown was Samuel's fourth against the Rams in the teams' three meetings this season.

If the 49ers made the victory sweeter, the Rams didn't linger over that point after the game.

"Our guys genuinely knew the previous six games, where we weren't able to finish, had nothing to do with what's going to occur at 3:30 or 3:40 when we kicked this thing off," McVay said.

"We always talk about being totally and completely present, having short memories for the good and the bad, being able to hit that reset button. Our guys did a great job of doing that."

Music from the locker room pounded behind him.

"I look forward to enjoying this," McVay said, "and then getting back to work." ∎

Los Angeles Rams owner Stan Kroenke raises the NFC championship trophy after the Rams 20-17 win over the San Francisco 49ers. (Los Angeles Daily News: Keith Birmingham)

HEAD COACH

SEAN MCVAY

McVay Finally Gets the Best of Shanahan in Comeback Win

January 30, 2022 | By Gilbert Manzano

Rams coach Sean McVay made a puzzling decision to put his last timeout on the line by challenging whether San Francisco 49ers fullback Kyle Juszczyk was down by contact with less than 11 minutes left in the NFC championship game.

While McVay was arguing with the officials about a possible fumble, 49ers coach Kyle Shanahan wasn't considering going for the kill shot on a fourth-and-2 from the Rams' 45-yard line with a three-point advantage. That was Shanahan's chance to hand his close friend McVay a seventh straight defeat and keep his team in Los Angeles for Super Bowl LVI.

"We were never thinking about going for that," Shanahan said.

Shanahan said the two plays prior and a dropped interception soon after the decision to punt will eat at him for weeks. Perhaps if Shanahan went for it on fourth down, then he wouldn't be regretting the missed opportunities after the 49ers held a double-digit lead.

"Thought that was the game we exactly wanted up until that second-and-1," a disappointed Shanahan said after the Rams defeated the 49ers, 20-17, at SoFi Stadium. "I'm going to be thinking about that for a long time, and then the third-and-2 on that next play."

Once again, it didn't matter how many aggressive moves the Rams made to add star players because Shanahan had the Rams where he wanted them and all he had to do to advance to the Super Bowl was make one aggressive move on the field.

"We had our opportunities and we didn't come through on those three plays, and after that it turned into a game we didn't like as much," Shanahan said.

Shanahan and the 49ers pulled the trigger in the spring by trading picks to draft rookie quarterback Trey Lance. But Shanahan couldn't bring himself to do it Sunday when his current starting quarterback Jimmy Garoppolo was on the field with fourth-and-2 from the Rams' 45-yard line and a 17-14 lead.

Plenty occurred after the 49ers took the delay of game and opted to punt, but that gave McVay and the Rams an opening to rally. McVay finally got one against

Rams head coach Sean McVay heads off the field following his team's win over Seattle during the regular season. (Los Angeles Daily News: Will Lester)

Shanahan to end a six-game losing streak, and now his Rams will represent the NFC in their home stadium against the Cincinnati Bengals for the Super Bowl.

As they say, it's never easy to beat an opponent three times in a season, but the 49ers had a 17-7 advantage heading into the fourth quarter. The Rams' pass rush had no answers for Garoppolo's quick throws with screens to Deebo Samuel and slants to Brandon Aiyuk.

Then Shanahan decided to play not to lose and gave McVay an out for his head-scratching decisions to burn all three timeouts with nearly a quarter to go in a tight game. Rams kicker Matt Gay made the eventual game-winning 30-yard field goal for a 20-17 advantage with 1:46 left in the fourth quarter.

McVay had his own game-managing blunders, but he had Rams wide receivers Cooper Kupp and Odell Beckham Jr. on his side – and a few lucky breaks. 49ers cornerback Jaquiski Tartt dropped an interception a play after Shanahan decided to punt.

Suddenly, the Rams had momentum after Gay made a 40-yard field goal and tied the game 17-17 with 6:49 left in regulation. Later, the Rams found their pass rush when star defensive tackle Aaron Donald got a hold of Garoppolo and forced him into throwing an interception to Travin Howard to seal the game.

"For the defense to be able to close it out, especially after the last time we played them," McVay said referring to the Rams blowing a 17-point lead in Week 18 to allow the 49ers to enter the postseason. "The way that went. There were so many great plays today by great players. Just happy to be associated with these guys. We have one more."

McVay praised Kupp's performance and sidestepped a question about finally getting the best of Shanahan, his former colleague when the two were assistant coaches

for Washington nearly a decade ago.

"The previous six games when we didn't find a way to finish, had nothing to do with what's going to occur at 3:30 p.m. when we kicked this thing off," McVay said. "Those are separate entities. … Short memory and reset."

Garoppolo's late interception might be his last throw as the 49ers' starting quarterback because Shanahan and the front office got aggressive in the draft by adding Lance.

Perhaps that decision could bring the 49ers another Super Bowl in the future. But they had their moment to do it with this year's team.

McVay bought Shanahan time to at least consider going for it on fourth down after he burned his third timeout on the challenge.

"Didn't think it was the right decision," Shanahan said. ■

Following a string of disappointing results against the 49ers, including an overtime loss in Week 16, Sean McVay led the Rams to victory when it mattered most, in the NFC championship game. (Los Angeles Daily News: David Crane)

SOUTHERN CALIFORNIA
NEWS GROUP

Los Angeles Daily News
dailynews.com

THE ORANGE COUNTY REGISTER
ocregister.com

PRESS-TELEGRAM
presstelegram.com

DAILY BREEZE
dailybreeze.com

THE PRESS-ENTERPRISE
pe.com

Pasadena Star-News
pasadenastarnews.com

INLAND VALLEY DAILY BULLETIN
dailybulletin.com

THE SUN
sbsun.com

Redlands Daily Facts
redlandsdailyfacts.com

SAN GABRIEL VALLEY TRIBUNE
sgvtribune.com

Whittier Daily News
whittierdailynews.com

digital first
MEDIA

Local Brand Leaders — Known and Trusted for Over 100 Years

As premium local content providers, each of the SCNG newspapers has a long history of editorial excellence in their own respective markets — forming a special kind of trust and brand loyalty that readers really value. Exclusive local content sets the Southern California News Group apart, providing readers and users with news and information they won't find anywhere else. From local elections to their home team's top scores, when area residents need late-breaking news, SCNG newspapers, websites and mobile media are their number one resource.